STRENGTHEN
ENCOURAGE
COMFORT

Prophecy Characteristics

And Guidelines

REVISED

PROPHECY

STRENGTHEN
ENCOURAGE
COMFORT

Prophecy Characteristics And Guidelines

Prophecy Characteristics And Guidelines
is published by:

SEEC Ministries International

PO Box 298

Coldspring, TX 77331

Revised 08/2017
ISBN-13: 978-1975686529
ISBN-10: 1975686527

For a catalog of books, manuals, CDs, and
mp3s contact us at the above address
or our email address.

seecministries.org
mail@seecministries.org
martygabler.com

FOREWORD

There are marks upon a people which will help identify them as being prophetic. Some persons, leaders and churches will not be seemingly as prophetic as some others. There will be individuals and groups that have "more of an inclination" to embrace what is prophetic than some others have. This book is not meant in any way to pass judgment upon any who do not embrace the various areas of the prophetic with the zeal that some of the others of us do. Rather, it is presented as the result of much research and observation over many years of relating to those in the prophetic movement. It is this writer's hope that persons who read this study will be inspired to see more prophetic possibilities and make themselves more available than ever before to be used more fully by the Holy Spirit in expressing the "testimony of Jesus," that is, the resurrected Jesus in a dark and hopeless world. The objective of doubtlessly evidencing a risen Jesus would, I think, include each and every believer. A good place to start would be to begin a journey of understanding what makes the "prophetic" the prophetic.

The prophetic ministry very possibly has the greatest potential for the glory of God's name in this hour and at the same time potential for turning people off to the moves of God at the turn of the century. Let us give ourselves wholeheartedly to purity unto God and unto one another in relationship so that "every joint" may supply to the "increase of the Body unto the edifying of itself in love."

— Marty Gabler (May 2003)

Prophecy
Characteristics And Guidelines

CONTENTS

Section One

Section Two

Section One:
Prophetic Characteristics

Chapter One
What Is "Prophetic"?

INTRODUCTION

There are marks upon a people which will help identify them as being prophetic. Some persons, leaders and churches will not be seemingly as prophetic as some others. There will be individuals and groups that have "more of an inclination" to embrace what is prophetic than some others have. This portion of study (and the sections about *Marks Of The Prophetic Church*) is not meant in any way to pass judgment upon any who do not embrace the various areas of the prophetic with the zeal that some of the others of us do. Rather, it is presented as the result of much research and observation over many years of relating to those in the prophetic movement. It is this writer's hope that persons who read this study will be inspired to see more prophetic possibilities and make themselves more available than ever before to be used more fully by the Holy Spirit in expressing the "testimony of Jesus," that is, the resurrected Jesus in a dark and hopeless world. The objective of doubtlessly evidencing a risen Jesus would, I think, include each and every believer. A good place to start would be to begin a journey of understanding what makes the "prophetic" the prophetic. Though this first lesson is lengthy, the author felt it best to keep this section of study in one body.

THE "PROPHETIC"

From study and observation that has spanned more than twelve years at the time of this writing, I would include at least sixteen things in the list of "what is prophetic": (1) supernatural visions, (2) dreams, (3) visitations, (4) trances, (5) words of knowledge, (6) words of wisdom, (7) discerning of spirits, (8) hearing from God through the various means that God communicates with man (which include all of the above). Prophetic communication is more than just saying words. In the list below, Glenn Foster shows us some of the ways that are prophetic communication. It would appear that from scripture we could include in our list prophetic (9) abilities like that of the sons of Issachar in 1Chron. 12:32 *men who understood the times with knowledge of what Israel should do.* (NAS) Someone who is prophetic (10) seeks God's ways (as found in His Word) as opposed to the ways of man and his traditions and institutions. That which is prophetic (and apostolic) (11) embraces and encourages multiplication of ministry through recognizing and equipping the members of the body of Christ. The prophetic is continually (12) seeing gifts and motivations in the members of the body of Christ. The prophetic (13) recognizes apostolic order, those who are set-in in apostolic order and honors their respective place of influence in their lives and in the life of the church. That which is prophetic (14) listens for, speaks and understands prophetic speech, e.g., *for unto us a child is born...* (Isa. 9:6). Prophetic speech is that which speaks as though a thing is already done; not just because that is the "proper prophetic way" to speak but because the prophetic eyes can already see it done and prophetic expectancy considers it done. (15) Prayer, praise, worship and demonstration will find place and expression among prophetic people. Though having already mentioned some of the vocal gifts, it would also be difficult to imagine anything prophetic without (16) all the gifts of the Holy Spirit being ministered regularly for the edification of all (cf. 1Cor. 12; 1Cor. 14).

In his book *Prophets And The Prophetic Movement* (Destiny Image, Shippensburg, PA, p.60) Bill Hamon gives us an idea of what the prophetic movement involves. "The Prophetic Movement includes all realms of the prophetic: prophets, prophetic ministers, prophetic people, personal prophecy, the prophetic presbytery, gifts of the Holy Spirit, prophetic worship, prophetic song, as well as expressive praise signing and dancing, pageantry and numerous ways of worshiping God in the arts and drama. Thus the movement touches on all natural and supernatural means of communicating God's word, will and miraculous ministry to humankind. It also involves the continuing work of purifying and perfecting the saints (that is, all believers) in Christ's character, as well as the activation of Church members and ministers into their highest calling in Christ Jesus."

"PROPHETIC," according to Michael Sullivant, includes things like supernatural visions, dreams, visitations, trances, words of knowledge and wisdom. "The fact is that no one can even become a true Christian without receiving a direct personal revelation from the Holy Spirit. In other words, no one comes to Jesus to be saved without "hearing" from God. In this most basic sense, all Christians have experienced a form of prophecy." (cf. Mat 11:27 – *to whom the Son wills to reveal Him,* NAS) Sullivant also notes that the prophetic is basic to genuine Christianity simply because it relates to the Word of God being made alive in people's experiences. According to the ancient prophecy of Joel 2, we can only expect that more people will be ushered into prophetic ministry and experience as the end times come upon the earth.

MANY FACETS OF THE PROPHETIC

In his book *The Purpose and Use of Prophecy* (Kendall/Hunt Publishing, Iowa 1988, p.25) Glenn Foster gives us some facets of the prophetic (although scriptures are in italics, quotes from Foster will also be in italics for this portion of study):

1.) MUSIC AND POETRY

Prophecy in song can edify and stimulate in a way that goes beyond the spoken word. In 1Chron 25 there is a long list of musicians and singers appointed to serve in the house of the Lord. Some of these were to prophesy with harps, stringed instruments and cymbals. The voice of the Lord is often heard in the sound of anointed music. Cf. When David played the harp for Saul, the tormenting evil spirit left. Music sometimes conveys marching orders for the army of the Lord. The same sound that quickens believers to rise and move out in faith also sends the signal of terror through the camp of the enemy.

In *Another Wave of Revival* (Whitaker House, Springdale, PA, p.55) Frank Bartleman shares the effect that the "new song" (cf. Ps. 33:3; 40:3; 96:1) had upon the congregants at Azusa Street.

"Friday, June 15, at Azusa, the Spirit dropped the 'heavenly chorus' into my soul. I found myself suddenly joining the rest who had received this supernatural 'gift.' It was a spontaneous manifestation and rapture no earthly tongue can describe. In the beginning, this manifestation was wonderfully pure and powerful. We feared to try to reproduce it, as with the tongues also... No one could understand this 'gift of song' but those who had it. It was indeed a 'new song' in the Spirit. When I first heard it in the meetings, a great hunger entered my soul to receive it. I felt it would exactly express my pent up feelings."

"I had not yet spoken in tongues, but the 'new song' captured me. It was a gift from God of high order. No one had preached it. The Lord had sovereignly bestowed it, with the outpouring of the 'residue of oil,' the 'Latter Rain' baptism of the Spirit. It was exercised as the Spirit moved the possessors, either in solo fashion or by the company. It was sometimes without words, other times in tongues. The effect was wonderful on the people. It brought a heavenly atmosphere, as though the angels themselves were present and joining with us. And possibly they were. It seemed to still criticism and opposition and was hard for even wicked men to gainsay or ridicule."

2.) INTERPRETATION OF TONGUES

A message in tongues when interpreted is equal to prophecy. Interpretation of tongues, like prophecy, is a message from God in the language of the hearer. Sometimes a message in tongues is a language understood by someone in the audience without an interpretation being given. On the Day of Pentecost when the disciples were filled with the Holy Spirit they began to speak with other tongues and there was no interpretation. In the crowd there were men from many nations who said, "We hear in our own languages these men telling of the mighty works of God." The disciples were speaking what to them were unknown tongues. But to the men who heard and understood, the words were prophecy.

I would like to interject a story of interest which relates to this point. During the Gulf war I read about an interesting incident which happened to a sergeant who was a member of the Assemblies of God. He and his men were awaiting orders at a designated position. While they were at this position, they were guarding some supplies. An Arab rode up on a camel and when he climbed down, he presented the men with a small bundle. He was apparently quite desperate. It was obvious that he was pleading with the American soldiers but they were unable to understand the source of his desperation because the man only spoke Arabic. From a distance, the sergeant was sitting in a jeep watching the proceedings as the man fell to the ground and began drawing in the sand in an effort to communicate. Something in the sergeant's heart was stirred as he observed the Arab's frantic efforts. He walked over to where the commotion was and asked what was going on. The men showed him the bundle which contained an infant. The sergeant then asked the Arab what he needed. The Arab responded with great relief that, finally, someone could understand him. He told the sergeant that the baby was in desperate need of milk. It just so happened that there was a large stack of milk in cases which the soldiers were guarding. The sergeant gave his men orders to load as much milk as possible on the man's camel.

After the Arab had left, the soldiers approached the sergeant in amazement. One soldier spoke up and said, "Sir, none of us knew that you spoke Arabic." The sergeant replied, "I don't speak a word of Arabic." With inquisitive looks, his men protested, "But, sir, we all heard you just speak Arabic to that man." The sergeant heard himself speaking English and heard the Arab replying in English, yet they were both speaking Arabic. I wonder which operation of the Holy Spirit that was. Perhaps it was the compassionate heart of Jesus enabling two men to communicate who, otherwise, had no logical way of communicating. So, was it the gift of tongues or interpretation or was it mercy or the word of knowledge or the word of wisdom or perhaps some other? The end result was that a person who has experienced the power of the Holy Spirit and speaking in tongues was able to communicate with a man who spoke a language which he did not understand. Why would we want to limit this Limitless God Jehovah which we serve?

3.) COUNSELING

Sometimes I have found myself giving answers to problems before people have shared their real needs. The Holy Spirit takes the things of Christ, THE Counselor, and quietly reveals His glory in simple answers that satisfy needs. Words of knowledge and words of wisdom can come forth in counseling.

A word of knowledge is something you suddenly know that you didn't know the moment before. Father is making a person aware that He knows just what they have been through or that He knows just where they are in order to give them hope for what they are now dealing with. A word of wisdom is a way out or a prescription for resolve of a matter. It is likely that a word of wisdom is something that was not known the moment before, although the Holy Spirit could quicken something to you that you learned from the Word or from experience in the past.

4.) PRAYER

There are times when I minister to people that I don't have a word for at first. I just simply feel that I am supposed to pray for them. As I begin to pray from a heart of concern and desire to minister, the Holy Spirit begins to guide my prayer and give me the things to pray for that the person is dealing with at that time. Sometimes that leads to a more detailed prophetic word. There are also times when I don't have anything in particular for the person so I begin to speak in tongues. After a time of speaking in tongues, the Lord gives me the interpretation.

According to Hamon "prophetic praying" is basically "Spirit-directed praying. Praying with natural understanding is asking God's help about matters of which we have natural knowledge (*Apostles, Prophets And The Coming Moves Of God*, Destiny Image Publishers, Shippensburg, PA, p.283). Prophetic praying is prophesying with prayer phraseology. It is praying out of one's spirit in his natural known tongue, flowing the same as one praying out of his spirit in unknown tongues. The prayer is on target and touches specific areas unknown in the natural to the one praying and uses prophetic motivation, word of knowledge, discerning of spirits, word of wisdom, etc. Intercessory prayer is much more effective when it moves into the realm of prophetic praying."

Prayer, Praise and Prophecy Work Together

The work of prophecy cannot be separated from prayer and praise. As a river flows from its source, so prophecy flows from the house of prayer and praise. The deeper we move into the river of prayer and praise the greater will be the release of the prophetic message in our midst.

Where there is a good flow of prayer and praise, the gifts of the Spirit operate at a higher level. The power of the Spirit flows out of prayer and praise just like a great river flowing from natural mountains. The gifts will function freely, normally, spontaneously out of prayer and praise.

5.) PREACHING

Prophecy can also be manifested while a person is preaching. There are times when an entire sermon is a prophetic word. I received a phone call a couple of years ago from a family I hadn't seen since high school. The mother called and asked if I would preach her mother's funeral. Although I spent some time praying about the message for the funeral, I couldn't seem to get a hold on anything. While they were playing a song from a tape recorder the Lord gave me the message. After the funeral I was attempting to minister to the lady whose mother had died. I was praying for her and ministering prophecy. Her brother, who had spent as much of his life in prison as he had out of prison walked up and, grabbing my arm, spun me around to face him. The marks of a very rough life were evident on his face. Angrily, he insisted on my telling him which family member had revealed the secrets of his life to me which had been the subject for my sermon. He asked, 'How do you know me? The things you said... you must know me." As I began attempting to explain to this distraught individual about the ministry of the Holy Spirit in such situations, several male family members managed to get him under control and remove him, under protest, from the funeral home. The Holy Spirit is able to bring THE message at the right time and in the right place, though the results may not be our brand of "ideal."

Chapter Two
What Is "Prophetic"?
Prophetic Actions

(For the purpose of continuity of study on the subject the author will maintain numerical order of the points from chapter to chapter as is necessary.)

6.) ACTIONS

Dramatic actions can be prophetic revelation. Sometimes a message is more clearly conveyed through seeing than through hearing. In Acts 21:10-11 Agabus receives a word from the Lord about what Paul is soon to face if he goes to Jerusalem. Agabus tied up his own hands and feet with Paul's belt which gave a graphic picture of what was awaiting Paul at the hands of the Jews. Not only did Agabus verbally proclaim what would happen but he also acted it out.

Lora Allison was in a meeting where she was not aware of what had been going on in the region. During worship, she began dancing across the front of the building as though she had a needle in her hand. She was dancing around all the leaders and pastors and acting as though she was sowing them all together. Later a person told her that they saw a golden needle in her hand and golden thread was in the needle. They saw her threading together the leadership of that meeting. There was a testimony that came out of that meeting as to the need for unity and what the Holy Spirit did through her obedient prophetic act.

A couple who minister all over the world attended a meeting at our home church, Grace International. I knew nothing about them. The Lord prompted me to throw my coat over them and speak of how He was going to cover them in future. They had been through much abuse at the hands of a local pastor and his church leaders. The Lord showed me in some detail what they had been through and spoke to them of the healing and covering that they would have in the coming years. That couple is now under the spiritual covering of our pastors and church leaders. They recently spoke of that day, of my throwing my coat over them, and gave testimony of the healing they have received under that covering over the last couple of years.

A young woman began attending Grace. She had experienced much consequence of sin and abuse. One Sunday morning our Pastor, Bill Traylor, called her up for ministry and began praying for her. Adrian, a young lady in our home church, received a word from the Lord for her. She took her by the hand and told her to jump forward out of the days of her past. She said, "Look back there now. Those days are back there and they are going to stay there. You are here now." The following week, the young woman shared the victory that came to her life as a result of the faith that arose in her through that prophetic act. I believe that as we are in obedience and participate in a God-ordained prophetic act that it is being matched in the spirit realm. I do not doubt that, as the young lady jumped forward in the physical, she was gaining a victory in the spirit realm.

PROPHETIC ACTIONS (MG)

CLAPPING HANDS & SHOUTING

Ps 47:1 *O clap your hands, all ye people; shout unto God*

with the voice of triumph. Clapping of the hands, i.e., striking one hand against another, was used to express joy (Ps.47:1) or exultation over an enemy (Lam.2:15); or repudiation: "to reject the validity or authority of" (Job 27:23 - ISBE). We can clap our hands to show our rejoicing in our God. Clapping could even be used with proclamation under direction of a leader in a meeting as a prophetic sign to reject the so-called "validity" of the enemy's actions within a nation or a city or upon an individual; the proclamation would be that the action and result are not being accepted as legitimate.

It is possible to offer clapping of hands and shouting as a sacrifice of praise (cf.Heb.12:12 *lift up the hands which hang down*). When one does not "feel like" doing or saying anything or when there simply is no clap or shout in one's heart because of circumstances one may, out of their will, begin to clap and shout as a sacrifice unto God. In Hos.14:2 offering sacrifices of the lips are compared with offering sacrifices of calves and is stated, "so shall we render the calves of our lips."

CRYING HOLY

Isa 6:1 *In the year that king Uzziah died I saw also the Lord sitting upon a throne, high and lifted up, and his train filled the temple. 2 Above it stood the seraphims: each one had six wings; with twain he covered his face, and with twain he covered his feet, and with twain he did fly. 3 And one cried unto another, and said, Holy, holy, holy, is the LORD of hosts: the whole earth is full of his glory.*

[Holy, holy, holy] This hymn, performed by the seraphim, divided into two choirs, the one singing responsively to the other, which Gregory Nazian., Carm. 18, very elegantly calls Sumphonon, antiphonon, angelon stasin, is formed upon the practice of alternate singing, which prevailed in the Jewish church from the time of Moses, whose ode at the Red Sea was thus performed, (see <Exo. 15:20-21>,) to that of Ezra, under whom the priests and Levites sung alternately, (Adam Clarke Commentary)

"CRIED": (Strong) 7121   qara' (kaw-raw'); a primitive root [rather identical with 7122 through the idea of accosting a person met]; to call out to

7122 qara' (kaw-raw'); a primitive root: to encounter, whether accidentally or in a hostile manner:

It would appear that the angels, in two companies, faced each other and alternately cried out to one another, "Holy, holy, holy!" with reference to Almighty God. They recognized that He is the all-powerful Lord of Hosts and that it is "the matter of our joy and praise; for power, without purity to guide it, would be a terror to mankind. None of all the divine attributes is so celebrated in Scripture as this is. God's power was spoken twice (Ps.62:11), but His holiness thrice." (Matt. Henry) The prophetic act in crying out or singing out "Holy, holy, holy" whether alternately or in harmony is reflecting the action and sound about the throne of God and participating on earth with what is in heaven.

LIFT THE VOICE LIKE A TRUMPET

Exod 19:16 *And it came to pass on the third day in the morning, that there were thunders and lightnings, and a thick cloud upon the mount, and the voice of the trumpet exceeding loud; so that all the people that was in the camp trembled.* 19 *And when the voice of the trumpet sounded long, and waxed louder and louder, Moses spake, and God answered him by a voice.*

Isa 58:1 *Cry aloud, spare not, lift up thy voice like a trumpet, and shew my people their transgression, and the house of Jacob their sins.*

Rev 4:1 *After this I looked, and, behold, a door was opened in heaven: and the first voice which I heard was as it were of a trumpet talking with me; which said, Come up hither, and I will shew thee things which must be hereafter.*

It is possible to sound out a determinate spiritual war cry when a congregation begins to release their combined voices imitating a trumpet. In Isa 58:1 the word for "trumpet" is "shophar" which means "bright" or "clear." "It was used for announcing the beginning of the year of jubilee, and for other ceremonial purposes; for calling the attention of the people to important proclamations; for declaration of war; and for demonstrations of joy. See Lev.25:9; Jud.3:27; 1Sam.13:3; 2Chron.15:24; Isa.18:3 (*Manners And Customs Of The Bible,* James Freeman, Whitaker House)."

LIFTING OR SWINGING A SWORD

Ps 149:6 *Let the high praises of God be in their mouth, and a twoedged sword in their hand;*

Isa 49:2 *And he hath made my mouth like a sharp sword; in the shadow of his hand hath he hid me, and made me a polished shaft; in his quiver hath he hid me;*

2 Sam 23:9 *And after him was Eleazar the son of Dodo the Ahohite, one of the three mighty men with David, when they defied the Philistines that were there gathered together to battle, and the men of Israel were gone away: 10 He arose, and smote the Philistines until his hand was weary, and his hand clave unto the sword: and the LORD wrought a great victory that day; and the people returned*

after him only to spoil.

Rev 1:16 *And he had in his right hand seven stars: and out of his mouth went a sharp twoedged sword: and his countenance was as the sun shineth in his strength.*

Heb 4:12 *For the word of God is quick, and powerful, and sharper than any twoedged sword, piercing even to the dividing asunder of soul and spirit, and* of the joints and marrow, and is a discerner of the thoughts and intents of the heart.

Eph 6:17 *And take the helmet of salvation, and the sword of the Spirit, which is the word of God:*

To draw the sword was a signal for war (Eze.21:3). It has been stated that "soldiers are men who draw the sword." Paul calls the Word of God the "sword of the Spirit" in Heb.6:17. The lifting or swinging of a sword could be a prophetic act showing our heart for spiritual warfare and our recognition of the preeminence of God's Word above all else.

7.) ART

A model, a painting, a sculpture, needle work, or graphic design can bear a prophetic message.

There is a community just north of Houston, TX called The Woodlands. On a main road through that area there is a statue on a corner. I believe the statue is prophetic. It is probably a statement to the people of that affluent area concerning their children and the effect that one generation's values has upon another. The statue is of a small child standing on the shoulders of a man. The inscription is a quote from Sir Isaac Newton and reads: *The reason the present generation can see so far is because they are standing on the shoulders of the former generation.* The generation coming after us should have all the revelation we have as well as the revelation that God has for their generation. The message to the present generation is that we should position ourselves to receive what God has for us in our generation in order that we may leave a godly and righteous legacy for the next generation to build upon. We are not just living for ourselves or for our generation. We must live as though there are others coming after us, no matter how determinedly some dispensationalists would wish themselves and coming generations off the planet. Our Lord Jesus lived as though others would come after Him and He imparted Himself to them so that they might, indeed, be....*these that have turned the world upside down*; (Acts 17:6, KJV).

The prophet Ezekiel was instructed of the Lord to build a model and dramatically demonstrate the condition of Israel so that she might realize her need of repentance.

Ezek 4:1 *"Thou also, son of man, take thee a tile, and lay it before thee, and portray upon it the city, even Jerusalem: 2 And lay siege against it, and build a fort against it, and cast a mount against it; set the camp also against it, and set battering rams against it round about. 3 Moreover take thou unto thee an iron pan, and set it for a wall of iron between thee and the city: and set thy face against it, and it shall be besieged, and thou shalt lay siege against it. This shall be a sign to the house of Israel. 4 Lie thou also upon thy left side, and lay the iniquity of the house of Israel upon it: according to the number of the days that thou shalt lie upon it thou shalt bear their iniquity. 5 For I have laid upon thee the years of their iniquity, according to the number of the days, three hundred and ninety days: so shalt thou bear the iniquity of the house of Israel. 6 And when thou hast accomplished them, lie again on thy right side, and thou shalt bear the iniquity of the house of Judah forty days: I have appointed thee each day for a year. 7 Therefore thou shalt set thy face toward the siege of Jerusalem, and thine arm shall be uncovered, and thou shalt prophesy against it. 8 And, behold, I will lay bands upon thee, and thou shalt not turn thee from one side to another, till thou hast ended the days of thy siege. 9 Take thou also unto thee wheat, and barley, and beans, and lentiles, and millet, and fitches, and put them in one vessel, and make thee bread thereof, according to the number of the days that thou shalt lie upon thy side, three hundred and ninety days shalt thou eat thereof. 10 And thy meat which thou shalt eat shall be by weight, twenty shekels a day: from time to time shalt thou eat it. 11 Thou shalt drink also water by measure, the sixth part of an hin: from time to time shalt thou drink. 12 And thou shalt eat it as barley cakes, and thou shalt bake it with dung that cometh out of man, in their sight.* " (KJV)

Chapter Three
Some Results Of The "Prophetic"

POTENTIAL GATES

We must be open to the various ways that God may want to speak to us in prophecy and use us in prophecy. All of the gates to our being have potential of helping us receive from God: the eye gate, the ear gate, the nose gate, touch gate, taste gate. I Jn 1:1 "What was from the beginning, what we have HEARD, what we have SEEN with our eyes, what we beheld and our hands HANDLED, concerning the Word of life..." (NAS) Ps 34:8 "O TASTE and see that the LORD is good; how blessed is the man who takes refuge in Him!" (NAS) Ps 45:8 "All thy garments SMELL of myrrh, and aloes, and cassia, out of the ivory palaces, whereby they have made thee glad." (KJV) I have been in services on several occasions when myself and others in the meeting have smelled the fragrance of the Lord. There have been times when there was a fragrance like perfume and times when the fragrance was like evergreen.

CHURCH SERVICES, AZUSA STREET AND THE PROPHETIC

You don't have to have a list of things to do in order to have a church service. Programs are not a priority. It may become noticeable that not all persons are comfortable in such an atmosphere and may require "someone" "doing something" in order to satisfy their sense of religious propriety. In *Another Wave of Revival*, (p.59f) Bartleman relates some interesting facts about the services in those early days of the Azusa Street meetings which hold a striking resemblance to a prophetic atmosphere.

"We wanted God. When we first reached the meeting, we avoided human contact and greeting as much as possible. We wanted to meet God first. We got our head under some bench in the corner in prayer... The meetings started themselves, spontaneously, in testimony, praise, and worship... We had no prearranged program to be jammed through on time. Our time was the Lord's..."

"All obeyed God, in meekness and humility. In honor we 'preferred one another'. The Lord was liable to burst through anyone. We prayed for this continually. Someone would finally get up, anointed for the message. All seemed to recognize this and gave way. It might be a child, a woman, or a man. It might be from the back seat or from the front. It made not difference. We rejoiced that God was working. No one wished to show himself. We thought only of obeying God. In fact, there was an atmosphere of God there that forbade anyone but a fool from attempting to put himself forward without the real anointing—and such did not last long."

"Someone might be speaking. Suddenly the Spirit would fall upon the congregation. God Himself would give the altar call. Men would fall all over the house, like the slain in battle, or rush for the altar en masse to seek God. The scene often resembled a forest of fallen trees... And the preacher knew when to quit. When He spoke, we all obeyed. It seemed a fearful thing to hinder or grieve the Spirit."

"Presumptuous men would sometimes come among us. Especially preachers who would try to spread themselves in self-opinionation. But their effort was short lived. The breath would be taken from them. Their minds would wander, their brains reel. Things would turn black before their eyes. They could not go on. I never saw one get by with it in those days. They were up against God. No one cut them off; we simply prayed—the Holy Spirit did the rest."

"We were obliged to deal firmly with the extreme case, but in the main, the Spirit passed over and moved out of the way irregularities without further advertising them. Many have declared we cannot throw our meetings open today. But if that is true, then we must shut God out also. What we need is more of God to control the meetings. He must be left free to come forth at all costs… Through prayer and self-abasement, God will undertake for the meetings. This was the secret in the beginning. We held together in prayer, love, and unity, and no power could break this. But self must be burned out. Meetings must be controlled by way of the throne. *A spiritual atmosphere must be created, through humility and prayer, that satan cannot live in.* And this we realized in the beginning."

"The Spirit dealt so deeply, and the people were so hungry in the beginning, that the carnal, human spirit injected into the meetings was discerned easily. It was as though a stranger had broken into a private, select company. The presence was painfully noticeable. Men were after God. He was in His holy temple, earth (the human) must keep silence before Him."

IS LIKE ISSACHAR

1 Chr 12:32 *And of the sons of Issachar, men who understood the times, with knowledge of what Israel should do, their chiefs were two hundred; and all their*

kinsmen were at their command. (NAS)

Prophetic people will pay the price in order to minister to their brethren. They will, at times, even have to stand in the face of the buffeting which comes against unpopular truth. Sons of Issachar will be able to see with prophetic eyes and wisdom that has come through anointed knowledge and ordained experience, and speak to individuals and churches concerning present and future circumstances. The Holy Spirit will use what He has put in prophetic people through word of knowledge, word of wisdom and through the molding process to advise, guide and direct members of the Body of Christ.

SOME RESULTS OF A PROPHETIC CHURCH

(A.) ATHEISTS IN LEATHER -- One Sunday morning, when ministering words of knowledge, Kathy noticed a teenager near the back of the auditorium. She was easy to spot since she had bright orange, purple and red hair. Not only was her colorful, spiked mane obvious but the numerous pounds of metal objects piercing various body parts made for a unique sight when added to the leather wardrobe embedded with steel studs. This particular young lady was considered to be most out of place since she was known in the community as "the atheist." Her given reason for attending church on this particular Sunday morning was that she thought the lead guitar player was cute. The Holy Spirit moved upon Kathy with a prophecy for the young lady. As Kathy spoke to her and revealed her heart and began to speak to her of the purposes of a loving God for her life, she began to weep. She accepted Jesus that morning. An excited pastor called us later that week. It seems that teenager, who didn't resemble the typical church-goer, brought teenagers to his door all that week so he could lead them to the Lord because she didn't quite know how yet.

(B.) RAZORBLADES VS. PURPOSE -- On another occasion I was ministering as the Holy Spirit led me to prophesy to some people sitting in a congregation. I had just barely noticed a sixteen year old girl who was near where I was standing. She looked like "death warmed over." There was no life in her face or eyes. The Lord gave me a word for her concerning His purpose for her life and how she would lift up young women out of the pit of despair and would see the Lord use her to restore them from drug-abuse and prostitution and from the damage of being physically abused. There was no response to the prophecy as far as I could tell. It didn't appear that she had heard or accepted a word I said. A couple of days later, the pastor of that church called and shared an exciting testimony with us. The young lady's parents were talking divorce and arguing in front of the family of four children. Their home was very disturbed and a very dark environment. This girl would light candles at certain times late at night and, in the secrecy of her bedroom, she would mutilate herself with razorblades. They had already taken her to the emergency room three times because she tried to commit suicide in recent months. At midnight of the Sunday I prophesied to the sixteen year-old, her younger sister knocked on her door. Upon being ushered into her sister's bedroom, the younger sister enquired as to the likelihood of her older sister mutilating herself or trying to commit suicide again. When the older sister heard the question, she responded in horrific disbelief. She said, "Didn't you hear what that man said to me this morning? He told me that God has a plan for my life. It would be stupid to try to commit suicide!" That night she and her sister agreed to become prayer partners for the unity of their home and they began their prayer vigil that same evening. Some two years later the parents resolved their differences and announced that the family would remain in tact.

(C.) FAMILIES AT BREAKFAST -- One pastor shared with me a story about a father who sits at the breakfast table each morning with his children. As they take time to sit and eat breakfast together, he takes turns asking each of his four children about their dreams from the previous night's sleep. As they each share their dreams with him, he interprets them. Some of them have been dreams which have prepared the children and the family for events which were to come in the near future. Some of them have been dreams confirming direction and decisions for the family and individuals in the family. It is reported that he also lays hands on them and on his wife and prophesies to them regularly.

(D.) PROPHETIC LEADERSHIP -- At our home church in Willis, TX we have an apostolic leadership team. Fivefold ministries are represented in that group. We meet each Tuesday all day long and there are occasions when it is necessary to meet on into the evening. Kathy and I are part of that twelve member leadership (husbands *and* wives) and meet with them whenever possible. A couple of years ago our pastors came to the meeting with very heavy hearts. Finances were way in the red, several families had left the church and there seemed to be a sly wolf among the sheep successfully working his plan of "divide and conquer." Our pastors requested that we all go to prayer for as long as necessary to hear a word from the Lord. On many occasions the various giftings in that

Tuesday meeting have each spoken from the vantage point which their particular gifting affords and the combined counsel the Lord has given has solved many problems and initiated valuable opportunities of ministry and edification. It seems that one sees a matter from the angle of one perspective while yet another sees something the other has not been able to see. We began to give the prayer request everything we could muster. After only a few minutes the word of the Lord came forth. The word was, "The anointing is on the instructions." As we considered the word it was obvious to us that we had left the vision and had amended specific instructions the Lord had given us only months before. Prophetic insight, discussion and the counsel of many (Prov. 11:14) got us back on course and within a few short weeks we began to see the favor of the Lord in restoring what had been lost in departing from the instructions.

Our Lord has given the prophetic to give us a distinct advantage over what the enemy has done or is trying to do. There are efforts on the enemy's part that require a response and there are people bumping about in an unsure world who require building up and direction.

★THE TESTIMONY OF JESUS IS THE SPIRIT OF PROPHECY★

The testimony of Jesus is definitely prophetic. Everything about the prophetic points to and glorifies its source: JESUS. *...for the testimony of Jesus is the spirit of prophecy* (Rev.19:10). I believe this scripture has two points of emphasis. One is that things prophetic put the attention back on Jesus and away from personalities or other emphases as the prime focus. Number two is that things prophetic reflect THE Prophet called Jesus and His ministry. Moses spoke of the One who was to come, *"The LORD your God will raise up for you a prophet like me from among you, from your countrymen, you shall listen to him.* (Deut 18:15, NAS) Prophet Moses predicted the prophetic ministry of our Lord. Jesus spoke prophetically throughout His ministry. He had knowledge of what was in men's hearts such as on the occasion when the Pharisees brought to Him a woman they had caught in adultery. It has been suggested that not only did He reveal their hearts by what He said but also by what He wrote in the sand (Jn 8:3-11), their hearts being so exposed that they departed the scene leaving the woman without any accusers. When Jesus met the woman at Jacob's well (Jn 4:6-29) He saw all she had done and revealed it to her with the end result that she accepted Him and brought her entire village to meet Him. Jesus also prophesied the resurrection of Lazarus (Jn 11:4) and foresaw the betrayal of Judas. That same Prophet is functioning in His Church today through many who have desired to be made in His Image and move in His anointing. Prophetic people edify believers and, at the same time, witness to powers and principalities that their Lord is truly resurrected from the dead, demonstrated by His ongoing prophetic ministry. John 17:18 *"As Thou didst send Me into the world, I also have sent them into the world.* (NAS) John 14:12 *"Truly, truly, I say to you, he who believes in Me, the works that I do shall he do also; and greater {works} than these shall he do; because I go to the Father.* (NAS)

The prophetic church knows and is totally yielded to the fact that God desires His Son to be manifested in this earth in this hour. *"Worship God! For the testimony of Jesus is the spirit of prophecy* (Rev.19:10)." The prophetic church longs for and dedicates themselves to be an active part of Rev.11:15 - *"The kingdom of the world has become the kingdom of our Lord and of His Christ. And He will reign for ever and ever."*

Prophetic persons know that the manifestation of Jesus begins in their bearing His image. The prime purpose of bearing His image is to speak as He speaks and to do as He does (cf.Jn.5:19) in order to bring glory to His Name. Prophetic people are directed by the Spirit and motivated by a great love for the Lamb -- not by emotion or desire for gain (cf.Mk.10:37-38;Lk.9:51-55).

Chapter Four
Marks Of The "Prophetic"
Part One

In this section of study we will begin looking at some of the marks which are an indication of prophetic people.

INTRODUCTION

The author has broken up this portion of study into four lessons while maintaining numerical order. There are marks upon a people which will help identify them as being prophetic. Some persons, leaders and churches will not be seemingly as prophetic as some others. There will be individuals and groups that have "more of an inclination" to embrace what is prophetic than some others have. This portion of study is not meant in any way to pass judgment upon any who do not embrace the various areas of the prophetic with the zeal that some of the others of us do. Rather, it is presented as the result of much research and observation over many years of relating to those in the prophetic movement. It is this writer's hope that persons who read this study will be inspired to see more prophetic possibilities and make themselves more available than ever before to be used more fully by the Holy Spirit in expressing the "testimony of Jesus," that is, the resurrected Jesus in a dark and hopeless world. The objective of doubtlessly evidencing a risen Jesus would, I think, include each and every believer. A good place to start would be to begin a journey of understanding what makes the "prophetic" the prophetic.

MARKS OF THE "PROPHETIC"

1. A HEART PREPARED TO BE PROPHETIC
EXPECTANCY

Matt 18:3 *and said, "Truly I say to you, unless you are converted and become like children, you shall not enter the kingdom of heaven. 4 "Whoever then humbles himself as this child, he is the greatest in the kingdom of heaven. 5 "And whoever receives one such child in My name receives Me;* (NAS)

We must retain the expectancy of a child and the believing heart of a child in spite of the persons and circumstances that have disappointed us in the past. The expectant and believing heart of a child might be illustrated in the following scenario. A child could be walking by a room where his parents are talking. The mother could say something to the father about a newscaster reporting an increase in the numbers of people going to Disney World in the past year. But because the child has such a desire to go to Disney World and really doesn't care anything about logistics or demographics or finances, his mind only picks up on two words: "Disney" and "World." That child will likely run excitedly out the door and announce to all of his jealous little friends that his parents are taking him to Disney World. The next stage of such an exciting drama would probably play itself out in the child's bedroom as he hurriedly packs his little duffle bag with a pair of pants and a shirt and the two peanut butter crackers left in a three-day-old package. I can picture him sitting eagerly on the edge of his bed dangling his untied tennis shoes, waiting for his parents to complete their packing so that they can come to his door and announce the time of departure he estimates is any minute.

PREGNANT AND BIG AND MISERABLE

When a woman is expecting a baby, it not only changes her life but it changes everyone's life around her. The expectant mother undergoes changes in her body, emotions and appetite. A woman who might not have been able to stand the taste of asparagus may now crave large quantities of asparagus dipped in marshmallow sauce topped off with a sprinkle of nutmeg; *and* she doesn't get such cravings until 2:00 a.m. Her schedule affects everyone around her. If she is awake at night, then the whole household may end up awake. The whole family may have been looking forward to attending a certain event but if, after arriving, she is miserable then the entire crew is affected by the needs of the one who is expecting. The subject of that which is expected is repeatedly made the center of conversation. The expectant mother's appearance, words and actions draw others into her vision in behalf of that which she is convinced is on its way in full manifestation. A prophetic mind and heart will evidence itself by relentlessly anticipating the fulfillment of that which God has promised. Js 5:11 *Behold, we count those blessed who endured. You have heard of the endurance of Job and have seen the outcome of the Lord's dealings, that the Lord is full of compassion and {is} merciful.* (NAS)

When a woman is nine months pregnant and has already made three trips to the hospital because of false labor pains and she is now in the middle of terrible labor pains, she cannot get up and walk out proclaiming her determination to have an end of the trying and suffering of birthing promise. The heart of faith, the eyes of the prophetic and the deep-down expectancy of prophetic promise will not get up off the labor table and attempt to get back to a former style of living. That woman may say, "I had a nice figure two years ago and I want that figure back!" "I have an urge to play tennis in the heat of the day." Or "I prefer to be mountain climbing at this particular time." *But* she has an appointment with destiny – to birth that which is promised. She will never be the same again. The true prophetic face may grimace and the prophetic voice may occasionally wail but it stays with the birthing process.

A heart that is prophetic is a heart that is available to God for prophetic adventures. Prophetic people have a heart to receive from God and then do what He said do. SAY: Prophecy is for ME. Prophetic experiences are for ME. I have a heart for the prophetic! Hab 2:3 *"For the vision is yet for the appointed time; it hastens toward the goal, and it will not fail. THOUGH IT TARRIES, WAIT FOR IT; for it will certainly come, it will not delay.* (NAS)

Cf. Hab 2:3 *But these things I plan won't happen right away. Slowly, steadily, surely, the time approaches when the vision will be fulfilled. If it seems slow, do not despair, for these things will surely come to pass. Just be patient! They will not be overdue a single day!* (TLB)

Ps 138:8 *The LORD will accomplish what concerns me; Thy lovingkindness, O LORD, is everlasting; do not forsake the works of Thy hands.* (NAS)

2. PROPHETIC PEOPLE ARE A DISTINCT PEOPLE

Prophetic people are willing to stand apart from the crowd. The Old Testament prophets and our various Bible heroes were not allowed the luxury of being generic faces among the masses. Not only did they speak prophetically but their very lifestyles were prophetic and out of the ordinary. Characters like Abraham, Joseph, Moses and Daniel are only a few who led lives of distinction. But God has desired a distinct people, as the passages listed below indicate. In the book of Acts, it was the church which was accused of having turned the world upside down (Acts 17:6) rather than one outstanding person. The followers of Jesus at Antioch were called by a distinctive name "christianos" to indicate their life and manner as imitating *the* Christ. Jn. 17:16 enables us to realize that our walk and our talk will be different from the world.

Gen 18:25 *"Far be it from Thee to do such a thing, to slay the righteous with the wicked, so that the righteous and the wicked are {treated} alike. Far be it from Thee! Shall not the Judge of all the earth deal justly?"* (NAS)

Deut 28:9 *"The LORD will establish you as a holy people to Himself, as He swore to you, if you will keep the commandments of the LORD your God, and walk in His ways.*

10 "So all the peoples of the earth shall see that you are called by the name of the LORD; and they shall be afraid of you. (NAS)

Isa 61:9 *Then their offspring will be known among the*

nations, and their descendants in the midst of the peoples. *All who see them will recognize them because they are the offspring {whom} the LORD has blessed.* (NAS)

Mal 3:16 *Then those who feared the LORD spoke to one another, and the LORD gave attention and heard {it,} and a book of remembrance was written before Him for those who fear the LORD and who esteem His name. 17 "And they will be Mine," says the LORD of hosts, "on the day that I prepare {My} own possession, and I will spare them as a man spares his own son who serves him." 18 So you will again distinguish between the righteous and the wicked, between one who serves God and one who does not serve Him.* (NAS)

Matt 5:14 *"You are the light of the world. A city set on a hill cannot be hidden.* (NAS)

John 17:16 *"They are not of the world, even as I am not of the world.* (NAS)

1 Cor 2:12 *Now we have received, not the spirit of the world, but the Spirit who is from God, that we might know the things freely given to us by God,* (NAS)

I Jn 4:5 *They are from the world; therefore they speak {as} from the world, and the world listens to them. 6 We are from God; he who knows God listens to us; he who is not from God does not listen to us. By this we know the spirit of truth and the spirit of error.* (NAS)

In these verses God has promised that His people will be a DISTINCT people.

dis·tinct   (Spanish: distinto) 1. distinguished as not being the same; not identical; separate (sometimes fol. by *from*): 2. different in nature or quality; dissimilar (sometimes fol. by *from*):   3. clear to the senses or intellect; plain; unmistakable: 4. distinguishing or perceiving clearly   5. unquestionably exceptional or notable

3. EMBRACES PROPHETIC COMMUNICATION
COVETS TO PROPHESY

1 Cor 14:39 *Wherefore, brethren, covet to prophesy, and forbid not to speak with tongues.* (KJV)

1 Cor 14:39 *Therefore, my brethren, desire earnestly to prophesy, and do not forbid to speak in tongues.* (NAS)

1 Cor 14:39 Therefore, my brothers, be eager to prophesy, and do not forbid speaking in tongues. (NIV)

COVET: to burn with zeal; to be zealous in the pursuit of good; to pursue; to exert oneself for one (Thayer)

One of the most amazing things about living in this age is that *we get to speak Father's heart to other people.* I have heard it said that Old Testament prophecy is revelation received and that New Testament prophecy is revelation perceived. He allows us to express the impressions, visions and thoughts which He gives us. We are allowed to express them through our personality and in our own words. What grace this is!

NOT ONLY WANTED BUT MUCH NEEDED

In the days to come, we are going to need all of the spiritual wisdom, knowledge and revelation possible to accomplish the Lord's purposes, and sometimes just to survive. Now is the time for us to mature in their use. (Rick Joyner)

As King David exhorted: "Let everyone who is godly pray to Thee in a time when Thou mayest be found; surely in a flood of great waters they shall not reach Him" (Psalm 32:6). Now is the time for us to build our houses on the rock of both hearing and doing His words. We are foolish if we wait until the storm comes before we start building (see Matthew 7:24-27).

On the day of Pentecost, Peter was compelled to quote a passage from Joel about the last days, in which increasing revelation was promised: "And it shall be in the last days," God says, "That I will pour forth of My Spirit upon all mankind; and your sons and your daughters *shall prophesy, and your young men shall see visions, and your old men shall dream dreams"* (Acts 2:17).

PROPHECIES, DREAMS, VISIONS

Rick Joyner: "One of the surest signs of a true outpouring of the Holy Spirit is an increase in the number and intensity of prophecies, visions and dreams. When the Lord pours out His Spirit, He increases His communication with us. Prophecies, visions and dreams are ways in which the God who is *Spirit* communicates with us who are *flesh.*"

WE SHOULD SET THE PRECEDENT

One reason Joyner gives us for such an increase of demonic activity in the area of supernatural experiences is to confuse the church so that she will reject the real gifts and experiences which the Lord is restoring to her. "Satan knows that these are essential to the accomplishing of God's purposes in this last hour, and he can be expected to do all he can to muddy these waters. The best way for us to help clear up the mess he is making is to find the pure source of the stream."

"We have come to the time of the great power conflict of the ages. The power of the cults and the New Age Movement is increasing dramatically, but the Lord has not left His people without power to face this evil onslaught. "When the enemy shall come in like a flood, the spirit of the LORD shall lift up a standard against him" (Isaiah 59:19 KJV). As the power of cults has been increasing, the power given to the church has been increasing even more. Cults have begun receiving supernatural revelation about Christian leaders in order to begin systematic attacks on them. However, the Lord has begun raising up prophets to discern the enemy's schemes so that the church can start ambushing him, turning his evil strategy into his own trap.

As we proceed toward the conclusion of this age, the conflict between light and darkness will become increasingly supernatural. The day when it was possible to take a neutral stance toward the supernatural is over. If we do not know the true power of God's Spirit, we will become increasingly subject to the power of the evil one. Those whose fears or doctrines have led them to avoid even the Lord's supernatural power will soon find themselves and their children easy prey for evil supernatural powers."

CALLED TO FILL THE VOID

Our God created us to have fellowship with Him and it

should be obvious that He is Spirit (Jn.4:24). According to John, the only way to worship this Spirit God is to worship Him in spirit and truth. Many have been drawn to the supernatural and to darkness trying to fill the void which should be full of spiritual worship to Almighty God. Joyner writes, "If this is *not* fulfilled by the Spirit of Truth, who leads us to worship the Lord in spirit and truth, we will be deceived by the spirit of error." The great writer C.S. Lewis observed, "If you deny a man food, he will gobble poison." "If we deny people access to a proper supernatural relationship with God, they will succumb to the oppression and seductions of evil supernatural power." (Joyner, *Prophetic Ministry,* Morning Star Publ., p.77)

Chapter Five
Marks Of The "Prophetic"
Part Two

4. SEEKS OUT GOD'S WAYS

So then, a prophetic people would seek out God's ways and means of communication rather than expecting God to come down to ours. Cf. *"For My thoughts are not your thoughts, neither are your ways My ways," declares the LORD. 9 "For {as} the heavens are higher than the earth, so are My ways higher than your ways, and My thoughts than your thoughts.* (Isa 55:8-9 NAS)

Also Cf. *It is the glory of God to conceal a thing: but the honour of kings is to search out a matter.* (Prov 25:2 KJV)

His superior (and without limitation) thoughts break into our finite (and limited) thoughts and are therefore empowered to accomplish His purposes. We continually demand that God fit into our paradigm and God is continually trying to get us into His paradigm (Cf. Phil 1:6). Do you want a larger experience in God? Then you must allow God to enlarge your revelation. We cannot operate beyond our revelation.

AN ADMINISTRATION ALREADY UNDERWAY

Father God is sitting firmly upon His Seat Of Administration in Heaven. His ways are above our ways and His thoughts above our thoughts (Isa 55:9; also cf. Prov 3:5-6). There is a Kingdom and an Administration of that Kingdom already fully intact. *He made known to us the mystery of His will, according to His kind intention which He purposed in Him 10 with a view to an administration suitable to the fulness of the times, {that is} the summing up of all things in Christ, things in the heavens and things upon the earth. In Him 11 also we have obtained an inheritance, having been predestined according to His purpose who works all things after the counsel of His will...* (Eph 1:9-11, NAS) HIS Administration is the only one which is *suitable* to HIS purpose which is to make Christ Jesus Head of all things and..... second to none.

It seems that men are ever seeking to bring this Great Administrator down to their ways and their thoughts, hence, attempting to manipulate His power and authority for their agendas and programs and purposes.... wherein God gets used.... not served.... not worshipped. *Seek ye first the Kingdom of God and His righteousness....* Seek first His "right ways".... His order.... and THEN all these other things which have not even been worthy of consideration in comparison to the superiority of HIMSELF and HIS Christ and HIS Kingdom and HIS righteousness, *will be added unto you* (Mt 6:33). Without HIS Kingdom (HIS rule, order, right ways, and authority) the end result is emptiness and no end to dissatisfaction. Without HIS Kingdom, we get the results that mere men and their drives and their agendas can get us.... or maybe we get the same results the Jews got from their Barabbas.... bruises, bashed heads, or even death. Do not be deceived — there is a blood-thirsty "Pilate" out there waiting and hoping for an opportunity to display *his* power and authority over those who willingly expose themselves to it.

Why does God speak prophetically and do things

prophetically? Why doesn't He just do things the way that is normal to all of us? Joyner: "He is not going to change to comply with our ways; we are going to have to change to comply with His ways if there is going to be communication between us. In the prophetic God is not just trying to tell us *what* He is doing, He wants us to see *why* He is doing it. God's prophetic ways keep us seeking Him and dependent upon Him."

5. RESPONSIVE TO GOD'S HEART
THAT WE ARE ALL PROPHETIC

"I wish that all the Lord's people were prophets and that the Lord would put His Spirit on them! (Num.11:29 NIV)" Well, He has! (cf .Lk.24:49; Acts1:4;2:4,16-18,31; 1Co.12:4,7,11,31) This was the heart of God being expressed through Moses for then and for now. Moses spoke the heart of God and told us that He wants a prophetic people. Joel said it's coming, Peter said it's here and Paul said we have permission. 1 Cor 14:31 *For ye may all prophesy one by one, that all may learn, and all may be comforted.* (KJV)

God's desire is for *all* to speak His wonders, to spontaneously speak forth His heart to people for their strengthening, encouraging and comforting (1Co.14:3). Both male and female as well as all age groups were included in Joel's prophecy in Chapter 2. It *is* possible for all to prophesy. That same heart of God expressed in Moses and Joel was also explosive in Paul in the New Testament.

The scriptures teach us that we "know in part and prophesy in part." (1Co 13:9) The part that is not prophesied is for us to discover through prayer while face to face with God as Moses met face to face with God. As a result of Moses meeting face to face with God, it was said of him that he not only knew the "deeds" of God but also the "ways" of God. That sounds rather complete as opposed to "in part." "Ways" in scripture have to do with "access." We have access to God's heart, voice and plans which include knowledge of tomorrow.

The reason the Wesley brothers were called Methodists is because they had a method and what a method it is. John and Charles believed that prayer and Bible reading lead to sanctification. That being the case, then please call me a Methodist. The prophetic minister must have a well from which he or she continually draws in ministry. The only stuff allowed in that well is what prayer and Bible reading put there. We must never speak nor set an example in any way that would cause people to think that prophetic words could ever possibly replace the individual's intimacy with God. Not only must those receiving words become more intimate with their Father but those giving the words must continually press into God. The more we have of our Father's heart in us, the more He can trust us with the detail and accuracy of prophetic ministry. The motivation in operating all the gifts is love and that love comes from intimacy with Father.

GOD SHARES -- WE RESPOND

God shares with us the issues of His heart and we carry them out. We were designed to bring forth the "thou shalts" of God's heart! Thou shalt conceive, bring forth and call by name (Lk.1:31). BUT HOW? Answer: Luke 1:35 *And the angel answered and said unto her, The Holy Ghost shall come upon thee, and the power of the Highest shall overshadow thee: therefore also that holy thing which shall be born of thee shall be called the Son of God.* Does this sound familiar? It should. He has already done it once. Gen 1:2 *And the earth was without form, and void; and darkness was upon the face of the deep. And the Spirit of God moved upon the face of the waters.* "And the earth was without form and void" could be the description of the lives of some people. "Without form" means "confusion, to lie waste, a worthless thing, place of chaos." "Void" means "empty." BUT when the creative presence of God (which a cloud represents as depicted by Gen 1:2) moves upon the deep and overshadows a lifeless womb, the empty places and the wasted, confused places take on meaning and become full of life.

Some may be asking as Mary asked: Luke 1:34 *Then said Mary unto the angel, How shall this be, seeing I know not a man?* When one only considers the present circumstances, one can only ask how can this be? When the Holy Ghost shall come upon thee, and the power of the Highest shall overshadow thee then one can say *For with God nothing shall be impossible.* (Luke 1:37) "Nothing" in v.37 is a word that we really need to get the accurate sense of from the original language. In the original language it actually means "nothing"!

Your point of reference may be like Mary's when Gabriel greeted her (Lk.1:26-29): that nothing has happened in your life over the last fourteen years. That is most likely the factor that set her to trembling. God's point of reference is: thou shalt conceive and bring forth now, no matter what the past has been. Your point of reference may tell you that you are anything but blessed. Your point of reference may remind you that, somewhere along the line, you messed up. God's point of reference is *Hail, thou that art highly favoured, the Lord is with thee: blessed art thou* among women or among men or youth or children. But we must have that experience, even repeated experiences, of the Holy Spirit coming upon us, filling us and indwelling us with That which is far superior to what we are just in ourselves.

IT RESULTS IN AN INTERCESSOR'S HEART

God shares with us the issues of His heart and we get involved in intercession. 1 Sam 25:28 .... *the LORD will certainly make for my lord an enduring house, because my lord is fighting the battles of the LORD, and evil shall not be found in you all your days.* (NAS) Intercession is praying God's prayer requests. In intercession we are prayer partners with God. We are not fighting our own battles or the battles of our choosing.

PARTNERS IN THE HEART = PARTNERS IN THE WORK

The prophetic church is able to see beyond the end of its nose and is able to be partners in that which is global. Prophetic hearts are moved by that which moves God's heart. They see needs in other fields. They generously give money and personnel to the work; such a church searches for the opportunity. Not only does the prophetic church on the whole support works around the globe but individuals participate physically in those locations. There is a "going out and coming in" that God can bless. Seed is taken out and planted while vision and motivation are brought back.

6. A LOVING CHURCH

Follow the way of love AND <u>eagerly desire spiritual gifts, especially prophecy</u>....everyone who prophesies speaks to men for their strengthening, encouragement and comfort.

He who speaks in a tongue edifies himself, but he who prophesies edifies the church. I would like <u>every one of you</u> to speak in tongues, but <u>I would rather have you prophesy</u> (1Co.14:1-5)." Also cf. *"But if an unbeliever or someone who does not understand comes in <u>while everybody is prophesying</u>, he will be convinced by all that he is a sinner and will be judged by all, and the secrets of his heart will be laid bare. So he will fall down and worship God, exclaiming, 'God is really among you!'(v.24)"*

The prophetic church will be known for its love. There are some who believe that anything prophetic is harsh and judgmental but Paul informs us that the prophetic gift moves out of the heart motivated by love.

"Love casts out everything that hinders the move of God through us and to us. Love is the foundation upon which spiritual authority and the gifts of the Spirit operate. It is vain to seek the gifts until they have this foundation to be built upon. The stronger the foundation, the more power that can be entrusted to us." (Rick Joyner)

LOVING RELATIONSHIP

Prophetic people seem to experience and sense rejection more than other ministers. Elijah crawled in a cave and "licked his wounds." How many people have been bitten while trying to pet a dog that was devastated by an oil pan on a fast moving Chevy? Truthful, loving relationships will help keep such extremes in check. If we are in the "regularity of relationship" Father can use those persons to prod us out of the depths of despair and on to fruitfulness. I cannot stress the importance of relationships enough. Our motivations and attitudes, which need to be checked consistently, will be noticed and spoken to by meaningful relationship. I am talking about relationship that has regularity to it — not hit and miss.

Perhaps it is because the prophetic gift is more vocal, more dramatic or such a desirable means of edification and confirmation that it is under such scrutiny. So many are blessed by it and yet so many are wary of it. Some want to throw it out altogether while others want nothing but prophetic words all the time. The first time I saw someone prophesy I knew that was what I was supposed to do. I began to seek God earnestly for the prophetic gift. I could hardly sleep or think about anything else until God moved upon me in such a way that I began to speak what I was sensing I had heard from God. It grew from a few halting words to, as many know, volumes at times.

I desire that others would not only receive prophecy but also that they would prophesy and experience the joy of edifying others with prophecy. When I received prophecy, it turned my life upside down and I haven't been the same since. Many people have told us in person, written letters, and sent E-mails telling us what God's prophetic gift has done in their lives and also in their children. But I also desire that prophetic people minister effectively, powerfully and be fulfilled without the many pitfalls that the enemy would love for them to fall into.

The prophetic ministry very possibly has the greatest potential for the glory of God's name in this hour and at the same time potential for turning people off to the moves of God at the turn of the century. Let us give ourselves wholeheartedly to purity unto God and unto one another in relationship so that "every joint" may supply to the "increase of the Body unto the edifying of itself in love."

AWESOME GOD, AWESOME LOVE, AWESOME

MANIFESTATION

We have got such an awesome God that He MUST reveal Himself. We have not seen enough of God revealed in this earth. He is *too awesome* and *too great* not to reveal Himself more than He has heretofore in recent generations. You can read your Bible from cover to cover every year but until that life-transforming, life-giving, delivering Word takes the form of manifestation, what have you got? (cf.Jn 14:12; 17:18; Rom 8:19;1Jn 3:8) God could not simply exist. He had to create. His attributes are seen in His creation. Ps 19:1 and 97:6 even give testimony to it. This mighty God is love and that kind of love requires love be reciprocated. The power of God, the presence of God, the Spirit of God, the essence of God, the love of God is so awesome that it must take some form to some degree at some level. God must reveal Himself through flesh (1Jn 3:8). *For God so loved the world, that he gave his only begotten Son, that whosoever believeth in him should not perish, but have everlasting life.* (Jn 3:16, KJV)

Chapter Six

Marks Of The "Prophetic"
Part Three

7. MULTIPLICATION OF MINISTRY THROUGH THE MEMBERS

The pastor will not be able to do it all. Edifying and encouraging is also the privilege of each believer. It will not be accomplished over the course of a week or two. Without the multiplication of ministry, the work before us in this end-time will not get done. There is a great harvest which we must gather in and it will be done in a concerted effort. Flowing in harmony with the "Giver" of spiritual gifts (1Co.12:11) actually should assure that prophetic ministry of strengthening, encouraging and comforting take place *whenever* the Body of Christ gathers. The Lord is present (and certainly not without power to minister and distribute ministries) even when two or three are gathered together (Mt.18:20). The "ye" in I Jn 2:20 is plural: *But ye have an unction from the Holy One, and ye know all things.* (KJV) Together we have an anointing or a divine enablement of the Holy Spirit to get the job done.

The person who ministers in the office of prophet is not supposed to do it all either; nor are we supposed to pray that a dozen or so prophets rise up in each local assembly so that all may be strengthened, encouraged and comforted. The prophet who does not equip the saints is no different from the pastor who has been accused of trying to build his own personal little kingdom out of his pastorate.

The prophet's passion for Jesus should incite God's people to prophetic expression just as the evangelist's passion for Jesus should incite them to evangelize.

JESUS MULTIPLIED IN BELIEVERS

Each of the five-fold ministries should find expression in each believer to some degree as believers are "prepared for works of service" (Eph.4:12). The gifts of Christ to His Body (apostle, prophet, evangelist, pastor and teacher) were not given as officious templates for mere perfunctory duty or display. Each brings his divinely given emphasis to the Body inciting, teaching and demonstrating (even activating) that gift motivation in order that it may be "caught" and emulated by each believer to some degree as the power of the Word and the life of the Spirit take root in their lives.

PROPHETIC IMPARTATION

We desire for the church to be evangelistic so we organize evangelism seminars and training. There are also efforts organized in going door to door for personal witnessing opportunities. We desire the church to be a teaching church so we organize Sunday schools and home Bible studies. The apostolic motivation is even given opportunity for expression in regular missions services or trips to a foreign country. Almost every Sunday of the year the pastoral heart is heard in the pulpit. The prophetic church will also present opportunities for prophetic impartation.

Without teaching and activating there will be no "prophetic people." Without equipping the saints, "preparing [them] for works of service," there is no prophetic church. Equipping, training and allowing opportunity for prophetic expression can be an energy and nerve-stretching prospect. But then labor rooms and nurseries are always needing supervision and clean-up.

PROPHETIC CHURCH IS NOT AFRAID OF AN OCCASIONAL MESS

Without messy labor rooms, messy bibs and messy nurseries the babies will not become "mature, attaining to the whole measure of the fullness of Christ." Cf. Prov 14:4 *Where no oxen are, the manger is clean, BUT much increase {comes} by the strength of the ox.* (NAS) The mature have the love and the wisdom to clean up messes.

I am of the conviction that whether or not the church is a prophetic church is directly attributable to whether or not the gifts of Christ pay the price to equip the saints. Paul loved the Church of his Christ so deeply that he had to describe that love in terms of labor pains, *"My dear children, for whom I am again in the pains of childbirth until Christ is formed in you* (Gal.4:19)."

NOT A ONE-MAN SHOW

A prophetic church is not a one-man show. There is no jack-of-all-trades. There is no little king with his little kingdom protecting his little throne -- while everyone else is merely acting out the part of funders, perpetuators and observers. Among a prophetic and apostolic people everyone is doing ministry; everyone is delivering, healing, prophesying.

Everyone is not looking for a prophet to give them a word all the time. Everyone is in the Word and everyone is hearing God. A prophetic people is not at a loss when a professional minister is not around to coach them as to what they believe and how to minister it.

Bill Hamon observes (*Prophets And The Prophetic Movement*, p.62):

"You do not have to be one of Christ's ascension gifts of apostle, prophet, evangelist, pastor or teacher to be a prophetic saint. Prophetic saints have one or more of the Holy Spirit gifts, ministries and other divine enablements for service in God's Kingdom. Prophetic people are those saints who have been educated, motivated and activated into their membership ministries in the Body of Christ."

"Classical Pentecostals and Charismatics believe they can biblically educate someone about the Holy Spirit baptism and then help pray that person through to speaking in tongues. They will even give them step-by-step instructions and acts of faith to take to activate the Holy Spirit gift of their own prayer and praise language."

"In a similar way, the Prophetic Movement is bringing the revelation knowledge, methods, ways and means of teaching, activating and maturing saints in their gifts of the Holy Spirit and spiritual ministries. I have conducted hundreds of special schools of the Holy Spirit for this purpose and have numerous testimonies from church members and ministers that it works."

"Ministers who are seeking to keep step with the Holy Spirit in His restorational work in the Church must begin activating the saints into their gifts and callings. We are called not only to purify the Church, but also to mature and equip the Church for the Day of the Lord. We are being challenged to raise up soldiers for God's army – not to prepare people for retirement and an eternal heavenly vacation as 'hallelujah hoboes.'

"Fivefold ministers are expressly commissioned by God to perfect, mature and equip the saints (Eph 4:11,12).

So we must train them in the use of the gifts of the Holy Spirit, our weapons of warfare. Sadly enough, for centuries Christian ministers have only sought to clothe the saints with their Christian armor (Eph 6:10-18). But the armor is not enough – it is mainly only for defensive purposes, to protect and preserve."

"The only offensive item in the armor is the sword of the Spirit, which is the Word of God. So the vocal, revelation and power gifts of the Spirit must be activated with the other expressions of God's powerful word for us to properly do spiritual warfare. This is the time for the gifts to become an active, integral part of the life and ministry of every saint."

EVERY JOINT SUPPLIES

Eph 4:16 *From whom the whole body fitly joined together and compacted by that which every joint supplieth, according to the effectual working in the measure of every part, maketh increase of the body unto the edifying of itself in love.*

The Word "compacted" means 'knit together"; "to cause to grow together." A friend was telling me about a man whose hand was burnt badly in an accident. This individual did not get proper medical attention for his hand and did not tend to it properly; the result was that his fingers grew together - maybe that's why we go through fire sometimes. Matthew Henry offers the words "orderly" and "firmly united" for "compacted."

One of the definitions of "joint" is "ligament." Dr. Reider makes these interesting observations (emphasis is mine):

"A LIGAMENT is fibrous tissue that holds organs of the body in place and fastens bones together. Ligaments are grouped together in cords, bands, or sheets. They are as strong as rope."

"A sprain occurs when ligaments covering a joint are torn or twisted. A sprained ankle is the partial tearing of the ligaments that bind the bones of the lower leg to the bones of the foot. Ligaments heal slowly. They may never heal if they are completely torn apart. Treatment of sprained ligaments may include exercise, supportive bandages or splints, or even surgery, depending on the ligaments involved and the severity of the injury."

(Bruce Reider, M.D., Director of Sports Medicine, Associate Prof. of Surgery, Univ. of Chicago.)

'If we want to be considered members of Christ, let no man be anything for himself, but let us all be whatever we are for the benefit of each other." (Calvin)

PROPHETIC PRESBYTERY

An aid to helping people along so that they may take their part in the local vision and in the Body of Christ is the prophetic presbytery. David Blomgren presents a strong premise for prophetic presbyteries (*Prophetic Gatherings In The Church*, Bible Temple Publishing, Portland Oregon, p.34).

"The prophetic word which operates today in a presbytery through proven prophets is likewise God's words. Their prophetic utterances as the words of God initiate a divine process to bring the prophetic message into effect in the lives of those so ministered over in a presbytery. The prophetic word that comes is a creative word."

"This is further illustrated by Paul in his first epistle

to Timothy: 'Neglect not the gift that is in thee, which was given thee by prophecy, with the laying on of the hands of the presbytery' (1Tim.4:14)."

"The gift that Timothy now possessed was given to him 'by prophecy.' This preposition 'by' I the Greek is *dia*, meaning literally 'through,' showing a channel. The prophetic utterance of the presbytery carried with it the creative power that 'gave' (not only just informed) or channeled the gift from God to Timothy. The gift was gien to him through the prophetic utterance and its subsequent, effectual work. This verse should also be joined with 2Tim.1:6 which shows the gift also being imparted through the laying on of hands as well."

"However, a caution must be exercised concerning this truth. One must carefully balance the causal aspect with the conditional aspect of prophecy to avoid taking this truth to an extreme."

AN EXPLANATION

In his book on apostles and prophets, Bill Hamon gives an explanation of a prophetic presbytery: "Prophetic presbytery is when two or more prophets and/or prophetic ministers lay hands on and prophesy over individuals at a specified time and place. Prophetic presbyteries are conducted for several reasons:

1. For revealing a church member's membership ministry in the Body of Christ.

2. For ministering a prophetic rhema word of God to individuals.

3. For impartation and activation of divinely ordained gifts, graces and callings.

4. For the revelation, clarification and confirmation of

leadership ministry in the local church.

5. For the "laying on of hands and prophecy" over those called and properly prepared to be an ordained fivefold minister."

REQUIREMENTS FOR CANDIDATES

It would be advisable to review the teachings of both Bill Hamon and David Blomgren at length to know how to set up a proper prophetic presbytery. This study is attempting only to introduce the reader to these subjects. A very basic portion of the requirements for presbytery candidates is offered us by Blomgren (p.79):

"The ministry of prophecy and the laying on of hands of the presbytery must not be done on an indiscriminate basis. Candidates must be carefully selected as qualified for this ministry."

"The Scripture warns against a careless handling of presbytery functions: 1Tim.5:22, 'Lay hands suddenly on no man, neither be partaker of other men's sins: keep thyself pure.'"

"This command warns us not to be in a hurry to lay hands on anyone. There must be due inquiry of their lives and the assurance of their qualification and readiness to receive this ministry. By allowing unqualified candidates to receive the ministry of a presbytery, we are excusing, them from the prerequisite basics which comprise a proper spiritual foundation for a pure and prosperous life and ministry. Because laying on of hands involves identification, we can become later associated in the minds of others with their sins."

AN EXAMPLE

For some years now we have been practicing a prophetic

presbytery at our home church. It has been used as a type of confirmation service for new members. Our pastor has a pastor's class each Wednesday evening. Newcomers are urged to attend the nine week class. During this period of instruction and information, our pastor shares what we believe and the vision of the local house. Persons who wish to join our church must attend nine weeks of this class. After they have completed the class and are certain that the Lord is setting them in this local house, they are brought before the congregation and before the apostolic leadership team. Each of the leadership team has been operating in prophetic ministry for a number of years, some for more than a decade. Their name is called, they go to the front of the auditorium before the congregation and the leadership team each takes turns prophesying to them. By the time the candidates reach the confirmation service, pastor is at least suspicious as to their gifting and possible place in the local assembly, and the prophetic word brings confirmation. The prophecy is typed out and placed in the pastor's file cabinet and he refers back to the file from time to time when places of ministry and service are in need of personnel. There are times when an individual voluntarily comes in for ministry or help or a person is requested to meet with leadership for instruction or correction and reference is made to the file to help that person use their prophecy to get back on the right track and "war a good warfare" with their prophecy (1Tim.1:18). Many have shared with us the value they have found in the classes, the confirmation service and the prophetic presbytery and the effectiveness of it all in helping them find their place of service in the Body of Christ.

THEREFORE, EMBRACES THE GIFTS OF THE

SPIRIT

A prophetic church doesn't just believe in the gifts of the Spirit. They are not merely listed in their tenets of faith, but they are practiced -- and not by an elite few. There is no such thing as a "ho-hum" attitude toward the gifts because the instruction of the apostle Paul requires we "*eagerly desire* spiritual gifts (1Co.14:1)."

In the prophetic church the pastor and church leaders are not so afraid of unruly individuals in the local congregation that they allow the fear to dictate whether or not the gifts of the Spirit will be allowed in worship gatherings. The church leaders do not shun responsibility to their Lord nor the flock in matters of church discipline. The pastor does not have to stand alone in matters of discipline and what is "in order" or "out of order" for he is not the only one desiring the ministry of the Holy Spirit in edifying the Body. If we are a prophetic church then the local assembly does not do without edification from the proper use of the gifts because of fear or ignorance of the gifts.

8. PROPHETIC EMBRACES APOSTOLIC ORDER

Prophetic people realize that the prophetic is only one of five parts. Each of the five parts complements the other (*complement*: Something that completes, makes up a whole, or brings to perfection.) The prophetic is a part of apostolic order.

APOSTOLIC ORDER is that order which recognizes gifts in individuals and recognizes spiritual authority in them, equips them and allows those persons who are set in by the Holy Spirit to take that place of influence in the church. Cf. 1 Cor 9:2 *If to others I am not an apostle, at least I am to you; for you are the seal of my apostleship in the Lord.* (NAS)

SPIRITUAL AUTHORITY

The spiritual authority which God gives is not recognized because of some form of promotion to a higher rank nor because of some democratic process but because of 1Co 12:18, 28: *But NOW GOD HAS PLACED the members, each one of them, in the body, just as He desired.* (NAS)

1 Cor 12:28 *And GOD HAS APPOINTED IN THE CHURCH, first apostles, second prophets, third teachers, then miracles, then gifts of healings, helps, administrations, {various} kinds of tongues.* (NAS)

"NOT DISCERNING THE BODY OF CHRIST" is with reference to each member's place in the Body of Christ. In 1Co 11:29 "not discerning the body of Christ" is with reference to the church, not the physical body of Christ. It doesn't say, "You're not discerning your sins". The setting of this context is a fellowship supper. This message is sandwiched between two chapters that teach us we believers are the Body of Christ. The result of failing to recognize the order of God is weakness, sickness and death.

JESUS UNDERSTOOD FATHER'S ORDER (And look at His results!) Here is the secret of authority: Jn 5:19 *Jesus therefore answered and was saying to them, "Truly, truly, I say to you, the Son can do nothing of Himself, unless {it is} something He sees the Father doing; for whatever {the Father} does, these things the Son also does in like manner.* (NAS) Jn 12:49 *"For I did not speak on My own initiative, but the Father Himself who sent Me has given Me commandment, what to say, and what to speak.* (NAS) Jesus didn't do anything unless He saw His Father doing it. He didn't say anything unless He heard His

Father saying it. Simply put: Jesus could be trusted as one through whom authority flowed. JESUS WAS SUBMITTED TO THE FATHER'S ORDER: Jn 4:34 *Jesus saith unto them, My meat is to do the will of him that sent me, and to finish his work.* (KJV)

A MAN IN AUTHORITY is the tantalizing subject we find in Matthew 8. But the principle in scripture is: that one must be *under* authority (submitted to and in accordance with) before one can be IN authority. The centurion in Mt.8:9 was able to order soldiers to "go" and to "come" because he was *under* authority, order, responsibility. There are frustrated people in the church today who want their gift recognized but have problems submitting to authority. Those people will remain frustrated until they change because "set in" authority is wise not to allow the character and attitude of such persons to be imparted to the people. When a person stands up before a congregation, they are not only putting out words but they are imparting their spirit. That soldier in Mt.8 might have a gift to direct the actions of others but if the proper authorities didn't recognize his character to handle it, all he could do is go home and tell his dog what to do. The gift would still function in a limited arena but the lack of character would prevent it having its purposed effective. The point of authority is not where gifting is tested but it is where *character* is tested.

NOT JOINED BY MEN'S METHODS BUT BY HOLY SPIRIT

Apostolic and prophetic people are not joined together because they were born in the same denomination but because they are joined together by the Holy Spirit for a common cause. Someone said that leadership is the exercising of influence for a common cause.

RELEASE AND OVERSIGHT

Part of apostolic order which prophetic people embrace is:

1. Preparing people for ministry.

2. Releasing people into ministry.

3. Providing oversight for those released into ministry.

Prophetic people must take responsibility. Relationship maintained and nurtured is responsibility.

WE ARE BEING PROVED

The question Jesus asked Philip in Jn.6:6 was so that he might prove Philip. *"He asked to prove him for He Himself knew what He would do"* Jesus was going to feed the 5,000 miraculously so He took the opportunity to prove his disciples. There was already order in what Jesus was doing and He was looking for some "someones" who were willing to come into that order and cooperate with that order and enjoy its results. Who will be able (or willing) to participate? Who has the capacity in their attitude and in their heart; and who is willing to submit to His order for what is about to take place? There is an order which is necessary for that which is about to happen. Jesus asked Philip, "Can you see my order?" He wasn't asking Philip to decide order but to see it and step in cadence with it. He wasn't suggesting that Philip come up with a way to pray. He wasn't asking Philip to pray and give Him some suggestions as to what He might do. Jesus is asking the present-day church to prove us for He knows what He is about to do.

Chapter Seven
Marks Of The "Prophetic"
Part Four

9. PROPHETIC PEOPLE HAVE PROPHETIC SPEECH

Prophetic speech is pregnant speech. Knowing that God's Word does not return void but accomplishes that for which it is sent forth (Isa.55:11) and that He is watching over it to see that it is fulfilled (Jer.1:12), a prophetic church meditates on the Word day and night. They meditate on it day and night because they need it day and night. They apply it to all situations of life both night and day.

Prophetic people speak to the mountain to be removed (Mk. 11:23) and because it is the Word of God, do not doubt that the "mountain" that stands between them and purpose will be removed. There is no attitude that says, "I'll believe it when I see it." Faith says, "Because God's Word says it, I can say it. I am what God's Word says I am. I am seated with Christ in heavenly places. I am predestined to good works."

THE LANGUAGE OF THE PROPHETS

Blomgren shows us some characteristics of prophetic language:

"The prophets' language included the following kinds of speech: riddles, parables, allegory, metaphors, similes, hyperboles, personifications, and others."

"One of the most outstanding characteristics of prophetic delivery is symbolism. Daniel is probably the most graphic Old Testament example. Daniel carefully shows that the symbols he uses are to be understood as symbols by the explanations that accompany them. The most graphic example of symbolism in the New Testament is the book of Revelation, containing approximately 350 symbols, the meaning of which may be unlocked when traced back to their Old Testament usage."

"In a presbytery the prophetic word may at times come forth from the prophets in similar language of parables, metaphors, similes, or the like. This prophetic language serves to convey more clearly in pictorial imagery what God is saying to the candidates. Other times the prophetic word will be plain and direct."

THE PROPHETIC PERFECT

An interesting observation about the tense of the speech of the Hebrew prophets is also noted by Blomgren:

"The Hebrew language of the Old Testament has only two tenses, the Perfect and the Imperfect. These two tenses do not entirely parallel our English tenses, which regard tense in the sense of time. The Hebrew people rather considered the completion or incompletion of the action as important. The Perfect tense indicated that the action was completed while the Imperfect indicated that the action was still to be completed."

"There was an unique peculiarity about the prophet's language. When the prophets prophesied about some future event, they would often use the tense of completed action, the Perfect tense. The prophet thus was stating a predictive word as an already accomplished event. This procedure was the result of the spirit of faith of the prophet, who was so certain of the fulfillment of his word that he stated it as an already accomplished event."

"One of the best known examples is that of Isa. 9:6 when he predicted the future birth of Christ, 'For unto us a child is born...' In the Hebrew the prophetic Perfect literally reads, 'a child <u>has been born</u>.' Yet this event would not be fulfilled for over seven centuries."

WEAPON FOR FIGHTING

The prophetic Word of God is a weapon for fighting the enemy of doubt or delay. *"Put on the full armor of God so that you can take your stand against the devil's schemes...Take the helmet of salvation and the sword of the Spirit, which is the <u>word of God</u>* (Eph.6:11,17)."* The "word of God" in this passage is the "rhema" of God. That is a "now" word of God. It is a word for this time period. It is an assurance from God and therefore a weapon against the enemy and his schemes. Whether it be a portion of scripture or an assurance which we received in the middle of the night or a prophetic word received from a brother or sister, we take that "sword" and swing it. It is not spoken forth once or twice but as many times as necessary over whatever period of time it takes until it gets rooted in the spirit of the one who has received it. Until it is spoken it is just so many words on a page or in a memory bank. It is not a weapon until it is spoken.

We speak forth the word for the prophecy that it is. We let the enemy and powers in the heavenlies (cf.Eph.1:21-22; 3:10; cf. Rom.10:8) hear it as we speak it into the atmosphere for it will remind them of *their* defeat in this situation. Speak it out so the enemy can hear it. Speak, for it produces fear in him and faith in us.

A SPOKEN SURETY

We speak it out so others can hear it and join us in standing on the word and in the testimony of the surety of God's Word. Abram was required to introduce himself as "Abraham: father of nations" years before his wife ever conceived (Gen.17:5). But because he knew God to be faithful and because he was joined to God in righteous covenant, he proclaimed the Word of God boldly.

Prophetic people do not just have conversation but their conversation is filled with prophesying, proclamations and confessions of faith. They and their words are pregnant, that is, filled with expectancy.

10. FILLED WITH THE WORD

A prophetic church is filled with His Word everyday, all day long for every occasion and every situation. The indwelling Word and the ministry of the Word is instant in season and out of season — apt to minister with or without a prayer line or a church service. They do not heed the false report. They do not walk by sight but by faith.

The truth of the Word out-weighs and out-testifies the facts of the present situation. The proclamation of the Word of God and one teenage shepherd boy out-weighed one nine and a half foot Philistine and his equally nasty army. The proclamation of the Word of the Lord out-testified Pharaoh, his army and a great deal of water.

Prophetic people do not act on nor reorganize their lives according to educated guesses, family history or prognostication. They do not jump to conclusions but seek the face of God to find out what *His* Word is on a matter. Once having received God's Word, the prophetic church stands on it *until* it is fulfilled. The prophetic church is zealous to see the Word fulfilled.

A prophetic word cannot replace the written Word of God, i.e., Holy Scripture. The principles found in Holy Scripture cannot be forfeited no matter how zealously a prophetic word was impressed upon us. One Monday morning a pastor called me and he was very upset. He wanted to know why I told one of his church members that she could get a divorce. In disbelief at such an implication I asked him what he was talking about. Come to find out, the word I gave her was, "You have a major change coming in relationships" *but* it was with reference to her relationship in the Body of Christ, her place in the Body and those who would fellowship her and nothing at all to do with marriage one way or the other. You would think that if the woman was full of the Word that she would have never considered the prophetic word to her as authorizing her to forfeit scriptural principle.

THE WORD AND PRAYER

I was ministering at a church in "a far away land." At the end of the service I was talking to some people I knew from having previously ministered at that church. Out of the corner of my eye I noticed a lady waiting to talk to me. When those folks left, she walked up, firmly grabbed my hand and asked if I remembered her. One year before, she had been delivered of some heavy stuff when I ministered to her and prophesied to her. She allowed me to know that she had gotten victory for a short period of time and also on a couple of occasions since. But this lady was really bent out of shape because of the general overall lousy state of her life. As she focused in on fault-finding I stopped her to ask one simple question. I looked her in the eye and asked, "During the past year, how many hours have you spent in the Word and how many have you spent praying over that prophecy?" She summarily withdrew her hand, spun around on her heels and departed. I surmised from her pastor's report that she had not spent time in the Word over *anything* over the past year.

We "know in part" and we "prophesy in part" (1Co 13:9). That scripture should plainly show us that there is yet a part to be known. Perhaps the part that we don't receive in the prophecy is the part we get in prayer and studying the Word. Prophesying was never meant to take the place of the written Word or our personally relating to God. On numerous occasions people have walked up to me after a service and told me that everything I prophesied to them, they already knew. But they felt it was awesome that God would speak to them in such a way. God was using me to confirm to them what they had already sensed was something from the Lord.

After having received a prophecy, an aspect of consideration is the matter of your prophecy being judged. The principle is found in 1Co 14:29. *Let the prophets speak two or three, and let the other judge.*(KJV). We have the Scriptures as the inspired, inerrant Word of God which all other words are weighed against. Prophecy in the New Testament era should be judged. If *any* word from *any* person does not stand in alignment with the inspired, written Word of God, none of it should be considered.

BECOMING METHODISTS

Perhaps we would all do well to become Methodists. The method that John and Charles Wesley had was: prayer and Bible reading lead to sanctification. We've got to give the Holy Spirit something to work through to bring about the completeness of His dealings in our lives. What's the best thing to give Him to work through? The Word. In fact that's the only thing He will work through. Phil 2:16 *holding fast the word of life, so that in the day of Christ I may have cause to glory because I did not run in vain nor toil in vain.*(NAS) ("holding fast"1907 epecho- to apply, to observe, to attend to; to give attention to)

Isa 66:2 ...."*But to this one I will look, to him who is humble and contrite of spirit, and who trembles at My word.*(NAS)

Heb 4:12 *For the word of God is living and active and sharper than any two-edged sword, and piercing as far as the division of soul and spirit, of both joints and marrow, and able to judge the thoughts and intentions of the heart.*(NAS)

If the Word is down on the inside of us, guess where the Spirit is going to be working. He will be working on that thing the Word is in.

Ps 119:8 *I shall keep Thy statutes; do not forsake me utterly! 9 How can a young man keep his way pure? By keeping {it} according to Thy word. 10 With all my heart I have sought Thee; do not let me wander from Thy commandments. 11 Thy word I have treasured in my heart, that I may not sin against Thee. 12 Blessed art Thou, O LORD; teach me Thy statutes.*(NAS)

If a person got away from God's Word (and that is how one would get into error), what basis would the Holy Spirit have for using them? Every believer must give themselves to prayer and the Word but especially those who desire to speak the word of the Lord to others and those who want to go beyond the limits of their past experiences. The Word is what the Holy Spirit works His works with in our life and prayer is that focused time He can do it.

BACK TO THE WORD

So much of religion is founded on mere *sentiment and *superstition which renders a cultural theology rather than a biblical theology or, as the words of Jesus so aptly describe it, *a house built upon the sand* (Mt 7:26). We've got to get back to the Word of God. Part of our task as a prophetic people is to get people transitioned from tradition and culture to the Word of God.

*sentiment: A thought, a view, or an attitude based on feeling or emotion instead of reason; Susceptibility to tender, romantic, or nostalgic feeling; An expression of such susceptibility.

*superstition: 1. An irrational belief that an object, an action, or a circumstance not logically related to a course of events influences its outcome. 2.a. A belief, practice, or rite irrationally maintained by ignorance of the laws of nature or by faith in magic or chance. b. A fearful or abject state of mind resulting from such ignorance or irrationality. c. Idolatry. (American Heritage Dictionary)

11. IS A PRAISING AND WORSHIPPING CHURCH

The prophetic church knows how to put the enemy to flight with warfare praise. Their mouths are always filled with praise. In our praises not only is the enemy made aware of the God who fights for us but *we* are also brought to realize Who fights for us. As we exult in Him, enemies are set to flight. "May God arise, may His enemies be scattered; may His foes flee before Him(Ps.68:1)."

We prophesy the enemy's doom not only in speech but also in song. We not only prophesy the greatness of our God in speech but also in song. The singing voice is the joyous voice. The singing voice is the victorious voice. Paul and Silas sang the praises of God, not until the jailer shook, but, until the earth shook. Their praises brought their liberty.

PULLS DOWN STRONGHOLDS

A prophetic church does not run for a safe bunker and begin praying for escape from the planet every time another threat comes from some despot in the Middle East. That church does not tremble and fret because its favorite political party is not in the White House. It is not a church reciting prayers while on the run. It is an offensive army on the march; taking territory from the "ites" and pulling down strongholds.

The prophetic church does warfare by revelation. A people who seeks their God for a battle plan will win the war (cf.2Sam.5: 22-25; Dan.11:32; Joel2:11)." *A wise man attacks the city of the mighty and pulls down the stronghold in which they trust* (Prov. 21:22)."

We wage war in prophetic praise and song and dance. We are commissioned to fight and our weapons are of divine origin, not of man. That is why we are so bold because we have *divine* commission and *divine* weapons that have *divine power* to demolish strongholds (2Co.10:4). Our weapon is primarily the written Word of God and then the encouragements He gives which are based on scripture. They may include a song in the night, a teaching, a prophecy or a praise song. The fact remains that the prophetic church is ever doing battle by being the voice of God on the earth.

LIBERTY

A bound-up church is not a prophetic church. If we are not free to proclaim the praises of God to God, how shall we prophesy the liberty of God to those who are bound? Events in the Old Testament are a physical example of spiritual truths and what was going on in the spirit realm. It is obvious from the Old Testament that the enemies of Israel were repeatedly thrown into a state of confusion and impotence when Israel praised their God (cf.2Chron. 20:21-23).

Knowing God's Word and knowing that He is watching over it to fulfill it and that it will not be allowed to return to Him without being fulfilled, a prophetic people cannot help but praise and sing praises and dance victoriously before their Captain. A prophetic church knows the outcome and cannot help but begin praising God even before the physical evidence.

A prophetic church is lively, active (movement), noisy, musical, has banners to display the greatness of God and the people's exuberance for Him in art and dance.

MARKS OF THE "PROPHETIC"

CONCLUSION

Prophetic people have realized and, in the past, embraced evangelist, pastor and teacher. Prophetic people have received from each of these and have caught their motivation and have made room for each of these ministries. The prophetic church also embraces the prophet and apostle. The prophetic church is willing to deal with proving prophecies though time consuming and personnel consuming. A prophetic people knows the Word and walks in the Word with assurance and makes room for prophetic giftings and prophetic people. cf. *"Have faith in the Lord your God and you will be upheld; have faith in his prophets and you will be successful* (2Chron.20:20)." The prophetic ministry very possibly has the greatest potential for the glory of God's name in this hour and at the same time potential for turning people off to the moves of God at the close of this age. Let us give ourselves wholeheartedly to purity unto God and unto one another in relationship so that "every joint" may supply to the "increase of the Body unto the edifying of itself in love."

Section Two: Guidelines

Chapter Eight

The Value Of Rank And Order In The Kingdom Of God

Don't take the message of this chapter and pass it over your shoulder to someone else. This message is for leaders and it's for everyone in the Church. There has been much talk over the last couple of years about subjects like "passing a way that we have never passed", about spiritual warfare and moving out with the presence of God to do what no generation before us has ever done. But the only way we can move out in the presence of God is in the order of God. It is very possible that the matter of rank and order among God's people is the last unrealized frontier to take before the coming of our Lord.

David's men of war could keep rank (1Chron.12:38). They won wars by keeping rank. They came to David at Mt. Hebron and they came with a "perfect heart." Notice three things about the men who joined David: (1.) They could keep rank; (2.) they came to Mt. Hebron; and (3.) they came with a perfect heart.

THY KINGDOM COME

Jesus taught His disciples to pray this prayer, "Thy kingdom come; thy will be done on earth as it is in heaven." He taught His followers to pray that prayer. I believe this is the way they understood this prayer: "Thy kingdom come, thy will be done on earth just exactly like it's done in heaven. Do you want to see the Kingdom come? Do you want to see the Kingdom come to your family? Do you want to see the Kingdom come to your church? Do you want to see the Kingdom come to the city? Then we've got to find out what it's like in heaven. Looking at the record of Holy Scripture, it would be impossible to say that heaven is without order. The Kingdom of God does not come without order nor does it function and bring its advantage and results without order. The principle of Ex 27:21 shows us that God expects His brand of order to be observed FOREVER (Cf. Lev 24:3,8).

Jesus' disciples were asking Him to teach them to pray. They might have been asking Jesus to tell them how He would pray if He were them. He made it plain how He wanted them to pray: "Thy Kingdom come, thy will be done. Thy will be done on earth like it is in heaven." I think we have a secret there that needs to be revealed for now. That secret is found in the preset order of the Kingdom of God.

THE ORDER OF GOD

From Genesis all the way through the book of Revelation we see the order of God. We see that the angels have an order. When we read passages about God and His throne we see that there is order about God's throne. We can look throughout the universe and see order. We can look in nature and see God's order. We can look inside our complex bodies and see order. Scientists, physicists and doctors, people who do research of all kinds, are continually awed by the order of God. Order exists for a reason.

The Bible tells us in Hebrews 11:3 that Genesis Chapter One is not the first thing that happened. Hebrews 11:3 is the first thing that happened. It's the first thing that happened that began preparation for your existence and my existence. Genesis chapter one is not the first thing to happen where you and I are concerned. Before the events of Genesis chapter one could begin to take place, order had to already be in existence. The kingdom of God is all about order, an army is all about order, a battle is all about order, an entire war is about order and it all starts in Hebrews 11:3. It says there that by the word that came out of God's mouth that He framed the ages. Before one flower was created, before one little caterpillar ever existed, before one beautiful butterfly ever flapped it's wings, the ages existed and they existed in order. In that order God began to place the elements of creation.

Every time in Genesis Chapter One that God created something He said, "That's good." When He created man He said, "That's good." When He created plant life He said, "That's good." When He created the fowl of the air He said, "That's good." When He created all the little animals that run about the earth He said, "That's good." And when He created all the supply that we would ever need, all the animals we would need and all the plant life we would need, He said, "That's good." Do you know why He said, "That's good?" Because plant life was created in its order, biological life was created in its order and animal life was created in its order.

LAWLESSNESS — THE OPPOSITE OF ORDER

One of the signs of the last days is lawlessness. Lawlessness is the opposite of order in the earth. Under a spirit of lawlessness, everyone rebels against everything they can rebel against. Criminals rebel against policemen, children rebel against parents, spouses rebel against the covenant they made with one another. Lawlessness will be rampant in the last days according to scripture (cf. Mt 24:12) and will continue to increase. Since the beginning of time man has rebelled against order, but we will not get the results we so desperately must have unless we come into order.

ORDER MAINTAINED BY GOD

It says in the book of Colossians "by Him all things consist" (Col 1:17). In other words, order is maintained by God. On a documentary I watched, a scientist remarked that if our bodies were not being held together they would fly apart in millions of little pieces and the same thing would happen to all the planets. If there is to be order it will be because we submit to God's laws and to God's principles. If Israel was going to move out of the wilderness, across Jordan to the land that flows with milk and honey, God tells Joshua that there must be order (Joshua 3). There were two reasons Israel was feared. The number one reason was "the little gold box," the ark. There could be seen the cloud of God's Presence and the pillar of fire. That was one reason why Israel was so feared.

ORDER GETS RESULTS

Even in that day armies sent spies to spy on the movements of Israel. And what the spies saw was this: they saw the order of God and the Bible says as a result that the nations that were the enemies of Israel trembled with fear (cf. Deut 2:25). God promised Israel that their enemies would tremble because of them. Enemies trembled with fear because of the order of God that was visible to the eye within the nation of Israel. God gave Israel order and their enemies trembled because of what order produced. The order of God was readily visible in Israel.

God told Moses to make a wilderness tabernacle that would have specific items in it; the items must have a specific appearance and be made according to specific measurements with specific ingredients. The tabernacle was to look a certain way; there would be a priestly order; there would be an order of bearers to bear the tabernacle and the furniture of the tabernacle. Instructions to Israel included moving when they saw God's cloud arise; then the tribes of Israel were to break down the tabernacle in a certain order and then march out in a certain order (Num 10:11-28).

When the enemies of God would sneak up and spy on Israel, their eyes saw incredible order among several million people who were all committed to it. Day after day they would spy on Israel. Month after month they would spy on Israel. Year after year they would spy on Israel and the order did not change, not for one day. The order remained the same. What God prescribed, his obedient people carried out and, as a result, the enemies of God trembled at Israel. Heathen nations, nations that had a multiplicity of gods, nations who did not believe in Jehovah, trembled in fear at Israel because of the order of the God in Israel.

JUST AS IT IS IN HEAVEN

The prayer Jesus wants you and I to pray today is, "Thy Kingdom come thy will be done on earth." It doesn't say on earth during the millennium. It doesn't say, "On earth while the rapture is taking place." It doesn't say, "Thy will be perfectly done when we all get to heaven." Does your Bible say what my Bible says? Matthew 6:10 is calling for God's will to be done right here on earth at this time, just like in heaven.

But it starts off by saying, "Thy Kingdom come." The Kingdom of God is the authority of God. The Kingdom of God is the rule of God. The Kingdom of God is the personal law of God that overrides every other law. If there is a law of gravity in effect and God wants something heavy to rise His authority says to gravity, "Give it up." If something like a bumblebee isn't supposed to fly, the authority of God says, "I am the Lord God of covenant of all the earth and you will fly." "It doesn't matter if you've got the improper aerodynamics, you will fly. This is my Kingdom and my laws are supreme."

The Kingdom of God is all about authority and authority in the intelligence, in the mind of God, in the righteousness of God, cannot be handled by lawlessness. Maybe we need to think about that for a moment. Isn't authority what gets things done? Nothing happens in government unless authority says it's supposed to happen. Isn't there pretty much a big list of things in the Bible that we are supposed to get done on this earth? Think about that list for a moment. In the book of Luke Jesus told his disciples I'm sending you out two by two. That's the power if agreement. It's the power of authority. Jesus said, "And heal the sick that are therein, and say unto them, The kingdom of God is come nigh unto you." (Lk 10:9 KJV)

The authority of God is greater than cancer. The authority

of God is greater than heart disease. The authority of God is greater than AIDS. The authority of God is greater than storms. The authority of God is greater than floods. The authority of God is greater than governments. The authority of God is greater than a medical diagnosis. Jesus was telling them that when you go to the people, do my works; and when you've done my works tell them the authority of God Almighty has come to them.

STEWARDS AND AMBASSADORS

The Bible calls us two things. One place says we are stewards (1Co 4:1). A steward does what his master would do if his master were present. The Bible also calls us ambassadors (2Co 5:20). An ambassador says what his master would say if he were there. So we've got a lot of doing and a lot of saying to get done, but it's got to be with authority. Nothing will happen without authority and authority will not come to the Church, authority will not come to the people of God without order.

Order is like a powerfully built box into which God puts his authority (cf. Ex 26:15ff; see v.17 "order"). The result of that authority is power. God is not going to put his authority in a box that's got a board hanging off over here, and a rusty old nail half-way bent over on the other side, and a broken board in the bottom, and a lid that is hanging off on one hinge. Are you beginning to get the picture? We must get the picture of God's order, not man's order. I'm not talking about just any preferred or recommended order, I'm talking about scriptural order. I'm talking about the order that was established in Hebrews 11:3.

God already has an order established. He's not looking for an institution to come up with an order. He's not looking for a denomination to come up with an order, whether it's an order they decided on or it's an order they adopted from somebody halfway around the world. There is only one order God works with and it's His order that was established before the world was ever created. Things are still consisting (Col 1:17) by the same order God set in Heb 11:3. You and I have been invited into that order. We are wanted in that order and if we are going to see the kind of results that Jesus got, we've got to come into that order. At some point and at some time, we must begin to do things differently than we have been doing them.

NOT RECOGNIZING ANY OTHER ORDER

I want to give you two very important points that are at the very root and basis of authority — two very important points that will help us get into alignment with God's order. The first point is John 5:19. "Then answered Jesus to them..." Who answered them? Jesus. Who's talking? Jesus. Now doesn't the Bible say that Jesus is talking? It's really Jesus talking here. Can you believe He's getting ready to say what He's getting ready to say? Jesus is getting ready to tell us that He does nothing outside His father's order. Nothing. Jesus binds Himself to the Father's order. Jesus recognized God's order and He never got outside of it. He stayed in the middle of God's order.

Do you believe that when the Bible says Jesus opened blind eyes that He really did? Do you believe that He really turned water into wine? Do you believe that paraplegics that never walked in their life got up and ran? Do you believe that the Gerasene demoniac that nobody could even chain down was set free of a legion of demons? So, you really believe the Bible? Do you really believe that Jesus and the apostles did what the Word says they did? Either they did those things or the Bible is a big fat lie. Jesus said, "You will do what I have been doing." (Jn

14:12) We've thought we would be able to do what Jesus was doing by screaming at demons. We've thought we would do what Jesus did by building a big enough church with enough people who had enough money. There are ministers around the world that try to make people think that if they send all their money to him he'll be able to do what Jesus did. But Jesus didn't say get all the money you can get together and do my works. Money helps; they don't give away airplane tickets. Hotels don't put signs on the front that say "All Christian Workers Stay Here Free." Money helps, but Jesus didn't say that's what will enable you to do what I've been doing.

The secret can be found in Jn 5:19. This is the principle we've got to come to. "Jesus said to them...." Now, are we clear who is talking here? Who? Jesus. "The Son can do nothing by himself." The Son cannot operate outside the order of God and expect results. Jesus was saying that the Son can do nothing by Himself but He does what is in the order of God. "I only do what I see my Father doing," He said.

ORDER IS WAITING ON US

You already know what Hebrews 11:3 says. God has already spoken order into existence. We're not building an order for God to come get in. His order already exists and has existed since before Genesis Chapter One. Some people think they are called to be a missionary. Some people think they are called to be a pastor. Some ladies think they are called to be a momma. Some men think they are called to be a daddy. Some think they are called to be an intercessor. But I believe we need to bring correction. We are called to find the order of God. When you find the order of God, if you are a missionary, you will get the results of a missionary. When you find the order of God, that moving dynamic, awesome, undeniable order will get you to the mission field. If you are a pastor and you get within the order of God, all of the demons of hell can rise up against you but they cannot keep you from being a pastor. All the demonized opposition within your church and outside it can rise up against you but they cannot keep you from succeeding because the order of God will carry you there.

From what Jesus said, He let us know that He did not come up with great ideas for His Father to do. In effect He was saying, "I do what I see already being done." Something is already being done. You and I are being invited to get in on it. There's an order and it's got action in it. Things are happening — things are getting done.... and if I can see them, I can join in with them. God didn't create the world then go off to a corner of the universe on vacation. He's active in His creation for the purpose of covenant relationship and participation with sons. Sons participate with their Father in His business (cf. Jn 4:34; 5:19).

The second principle is in John 12:49. Jesus is talking again. Really, it is Jesus. He said, "I have not spoken of myself but the Father, which sent me, gave me a commandment. He told me what to say. I'm not saying anything my Father didn't tell me to say." Are you beginning to realize why we are not getting the results that come from authority? Maybe, just maybe, we are out of order. Maybe we haven't discovered God's order because if we had discovered God's order we would be able to do the things God has told us to do. Sometimes somebody gets healed, not very often. Yet the Bible says that all who came to Jesus, Jesus healed them (Mt 12:15). We must submit to God's order so God can allow us to function with His authority so we can get the results that Jesus got so the sick can get healed, the captive can be delivered, and glory can be given to God's Name.

Order is waiting on us. We aren't supposed to be waiting on order. That which is already in existence and functioning properly and getting results is to be searched out. Perhaps if we stop praying for order to come to us to enhance what we are doing (and who we are) and we find out how to come into order, we will see and hear the things Jesus saw and heard. But in coming into order, we must be open to and accept what already exists in that order. Order isn't coming to adjust to us. We are coming into order so that we can adjust to it.

The Sons of Thunder, James and John, were with Jesus one day and the Samaritans were saying things, making remarks. And the Sons of Thunder, who were supposed to be seeing what the Father is doing and were supposed to be listening to what the Father was saying, said to Jesus, "Let us call fire down on their heads!" Does that sound familiar? Boy, if God would get out of the way I could take care of a lot of people. But then no one is healed. So often when we pray for people to be free from demons, it is like the demons respond, "Ha! Ha! Ha! Are you talking to me? Ha! Ha! Ha! Paul I've heard of, and Jesus I've heard of, but what kind of funny person are you?" You know how many demons laughed at Jesus? None. And He's the one who said I will do nothing outside of God's order.

THE KEY

You know what brings us to the order of God? The key to the whole thing is in I Chron. 12:38. Before we get to verse 38, there's a whole list of tribes that have come to

David. The discerning and prophetic tribe of Issachar joined David. They knew what Israel ought to do for the times. There is something most unusual which is noted in v.32. The curious note in that verse tells us that "all their brethren were at their commandment." There is proof right there that there were no people from the tribe of Issachar in the United States. If there is any one thing that you could speedily be reminded of in a North American church, it is that no one is at the commandment of anyone.

We have spent inestimable millions in the Church on teaching people to lead but how much have we spent on teaching people to follow? North America and her denominations and religious institutions are crammed and packed with people who have trained to lead but find themselves useless baggage in an ever-expanding miasma of self-will and lawlessness. Giving instruction and direction in such an atmosphere is very difficult and, many times, quite fruitless. Yet part of rank and order, in any army anywhere in history, is the factor of some leader at some point giving commandments. Recent church history would indicate that a lack of trust and persons who cannot be trusted abound, yet we cannot simply dismiss the principle of rank and order (and the instruction and commandment which accompany it). Any principle of God that becomes an option becomes a notable point of failure no matter what excuse or justification we contrive. Let us be careful lest we excuse and justify the flock of God into fruitlessness and failure because some of us did not have the courage to stand in the face of the buffeting which comes against unpopular truth.

This point may be the one stickler that prevents many persons from ever realizing the tremendous peace and fruitfulness of being in rank and order. There are people who want the benefit of rank and order without actually having to comply with the implications of rank and order. In the face of such a shifting wind, commandments and instruction become little more than carefully worded suggestions which in turn have become worthless prattle placating sensitive givers and attenders. We would do well to look around and honestly admit what we have produced and are living with….. and at what cost? Perhaps once we realize the high cost we will admit our lawlessness and forsake it.

ORDER AND COVENANT — ONE WITHOUT THE OTHER?

Another of the tribes which joined David at Mt. Hebron was the tribe of Zebulun. His name means "habitation; exalted" (Brown-Driver-Briggs). By inference his name represents fidelity (cf. Gen. 30:20). There were people joining David who were looking for habitation and who had an inclination to remain faithful.

The place they all willingly came to was called "Hebron." Hebron means "league" or "confederacy." When we form a league or confederacy we have entered into "an alliance between persons, parties, states, etc., for some purpose" (WUD). They made an alliance with one another and with David for a purpose: to make David king. Is there not a cause? They came there with a "perfect heart" (v.38). That perfect heart is a "covenant-keeping heart" (B-D-B). Personal agendas must die in order that the alliance may produce that for which it was formed. The "covenant" aspect of getting into order means that we stay around long enough to find out what we are in the alliance even after we have found out what we are not. We must stay in covenant long enough to see something bear fruit.

EXCUSES, PROBLEMS AND THE ORDER OF GOD

The men who joined David to help bring the kingdom had personal problems. These are not popular Christians who have just come off the road doing great victory crusades. *And everyone who was in distress, and everyone who was in debt, and everyone who was discontented, gathered to him; and he became captain over them. Now there were about four hundred men with him.* (1 Sam 22:2 NAS) They were going to take the kingdom for David. They were going to be the kingdom David was going to rule over. In the Old Testament, David is a picture of the New Testament Christ. We are helping to bring the Kingdom that the New Testament David is going to rule over.

All of the distressed people, all of the people in debt and all of the discontented people can be part of Kingdom function just by getting into order. If we all get into God's order we should most likely find that the things in us which have caused our distress, debt and discontentment will have to adjust to the working of that order within our lives (cf. Ps 92:13 *Those that be planted in the house of the Lord shall flourish...*). Personal problems do not excuse us nor exempt us from the mandate to get into rank and order. There is proof positive in 1 Chron. 12 that it is possible to discover one's place in rank and order while one is held tightly in the grip of personal problems. Heaven is not the only place where it is God's will for order to exist and have its effect. A victorious people of God (who just may happen to have personal problems) are supposed to be taking ground. I have read inspiring stories and heard the old-timers talk about soldiers who kept fighting and helping their wounded comrades when they were wounded themselves.

Have you ever watched small boys play soccer?

Wherever the ball is, that is where the entire group is. There is no order. You can't see the ball but you know its there because there is this group of competitive, striving, tunnel-vision want-a-be's everywhere the ball is. Yet each parent is so proud of their child and they excitedly cheer them on though there is little or no result. But they and the boys are excited because, at least, there is a lot of movement on the field and the appearance of worthwhile effort. The kids are so immature that the hows and wherefores of the order of the game cannot even be grasped. The problem is that everyone is trying to do the same thing at the same time and the precious few results obtained are only accidental. But when those kids mature and can understand the wonderful results of rank and order (being where they are supposed to be, doing what they are supposed to do) it becomes a whole new ball game.

The mature man of stature spoken of in Eph 4:11-16 is the Christ-man that has come to rank and order. The result of rank and order is that the saints will do the work of the ministry, we won't be tossed to and fro, every joint will supply and the harvest will be brought in without waste.

Chapter Nine

Why We Need The Prophetic

Prophets are not more spiritual than pastors. That's not why we bring them into the local house. Prophets are brought in by the local pastor to complement ("complement": *something that fills up, completes, or makes perfect* - Webster; cf. Eph 4:12) his or her ministry gifts.

Any one of the five-fold ministry gifts will complement any and all of the others. Eph 3:10 speaks of "the manifold wisdom of God." This is the "many-faceted" wisdom of God. Just as a diamond has many facets to it and you see something different each degree you turn the diamond, so it is with each of the five-fold ministry gifts. Each has something to offer that makes up the whole and we do not have the whole without each providing its part. The prophetic minister is needed just as the teacher or evangelist is needed to add their portion to the Body of Christ.

I. REASON ONE: GOD SAID SO

A. GOD HATH SET SOME

The main reason we need the prophetic is because GOD SAID we need the prophetic. 1 Cor 12:28 *And GOD HATH SET some in the church, first apostles, secondarily prophets, thirdly teachers, after that miracles, then gifts of healings, helps, governments, diversities of tongues.* God has set (set: to fix, establish, set forth, to ordain - Thayer) prophets in the church just as He has set pastors and teachers in the church. God Himself has established the need for prophetic ministry.

B. THE EXTENT OF GOD'S DESIRE

Moses, God's prophet, was only expressing the thoughts of God when he said, "...would God that all the LORD's people were prophets, and that the LORD would put his spirit upon them!" (Num 11:29). This shows us the extent of God's desire. He not only wants us to have a few prophets scattered here and there, He wants a prophetic people! Joel agrees in Joel 2:28, Peter agrees in Acts 2:17-18 and Paul concurs in 1Co 14:1,39. Others who established the need for prophets were Ezra (2Chron 20:20), Amos (Amos 3:7) and Luke (Acts 3:20-21).

II. REASON TWO: JESUS SAID SO

Another reason we need the prophetic active in the Body of Christ is because JESUS SAID SO. Matt 23:34 *Wherefore, behold, I SEND UNTO YOU PROPHETS, and wise men, and scribes: and some of them ye shall kill and crucify; and some of them shall ye scourge in your synagogues, and persecute them from city to city.*

A. HOLD ON TO THAT WHICH IS GOOD

Even though God hath set some in the church and Jesus Himself (THE Prophet) has sent us prophets, one of the warnings continually sounded is: "Jesus warned us about false prophets in the last days." This warning has been used by some as an excuse to reject all prophetic ministry. The reasoning is that if there are false prophets then all who call themselves prophets, or who minister in a fashion which could be identified as something prophetic, should be rejected as not being biblical for today.

Proper reasoning would lead us to understand that in order for false prophets to exist in the last days, true prophets would have to exist. Bankers, grocery clerks and retailers do not concern themselves with $4.00 bills. They are immediately unacceptable. There are no false $4.00 bills because there are no true $4.00 bills. But retailers take the time to examine $50.00 bills. The only reason there can be false $50.00 bills is because there are real $50.00 bills.

We are taught a good principle in 1Thess 5:21. We are taught to test all things but we are also taught in that same scripture to hold on to that which is good. Just because you bit into a bad piece of fruit once does not mean that you are never to eat fruit again.

John Blattner said that, in his experience, "false prophecy" is quite rare and that we should be very careful about labeling people "false prophets." He has found that it is more often what he calls "non-prophecy": a message whose content may be perfectly acceptable but whose source lies more in the speaker's spirit than in the Lord's. (*Equipping The Saints Magazine*, Fall 1989, p.15)

B. DON'T THROW OUT THE BABY WITH THE WASH

There are pastors who have "thrown out the baby with the wash" where prophets and prophecy are concerned. One pastor I know wants nothing to do with prophecy and it is not because he can't find it in scripture. The reason he wants nothing to do with it (and therefore does not allow it) is because he had a couple come into his church and try to take over the church by manipulating the congregation through so-called "prophecy." There was a lot of hurt and damage done. One of the problems was that he had done no teaching nor demonstrating of the true in order for the congregation to have the proper comparison. When I was a child I ate at homes of friends who thought their mom's cooking was just fine. I was barely able to eat it. My taste buds and my stomach were offended. My Mom truly was a great cook and I was hardly able to get down the terrible tasting food other kids thought was just fine. But I didn't quit eating because some people put food on their table that was offensive.

C. ZEALOUS IN JUDGING

Some folks have gone through great trauma trying to apply the "judging" instruction of 1Co 14:29. "Let the prophets speak two or three, and let the other judge." There have been well-meaning persons hurt and even churches split over zealous attempts to carry out that passage. I have found that in most cases where the gifts of the Spirit are taught and practiced, that when a word goes forth which is only of that person's spirit, there is an automatic awareness and acknowledgment by the congregation. The atmosphere will ring with the truth or the falsity of the presentation. Therefore, the type of reaction or lack of reaction is a judgment upon that word. Notice I just said, "upon that word" not upon that person. Our zealousness can sometimes put us in an "attack mode" that serves no good purpose. (Been there. Done that. Got a T-Shirt.) However, there are times that pastors and elders need to call persons in to wisely and lovingly deal with them. I do not believe a pastor should do that without witnesses such as elders and/or locally recognized ministers.

D. MAINTAINING PROPER FOCUS

John Wesley had seen a great move of God. It seemed to go the way of most moves of God because of the human element that can't keep its hands off. When it had begun to die down John Wesley prayed, "Oh, Lord send us the old revival, without the defects; but if this cannot be, send it with all its defects."

In a move of God, especially where it concerns the prophetic, there are those who focus so intently on the possibility of error that they miss the good. There is such a zeroing-in on the tares that the wheat almost goes unnoticed. The pastor at the Airport church in Toronto, John Arnott, has been asked about the "negative aspects" of revival and some of the things he has had to deal with over the last couple of years. "There's always going to be some fleshly enthusiasm," he said. "I would rather contend with a little fleshly zeal than carnal resistance." (Charisma Magazine, Jan.1994)

E. STEADYING THE ARK

Throughout church history whenever the presence of God was not allowed to prevail, men had to come up with ways and means of handling men and "steadying the ark." Men's ways and means have historically stifled the move of God. We have it recorded for us that when the Holy Spirit moved powerfully at Azusa street He handled quite adequately what so many churchmen fear - the flesh.

There is a record of that move of God entitled Another Wave of Revival (Whitaker House). Frank Bartleman reports:

"We thought only of obeying God. In fact, there was an atmosphere of God there that forbade anyone but a fool from attempting to put himself forward without the real anointing - and such did not last long. The meetings were controlled by the Spirit, from the throne.... Presumptuous men would sometimes come among us... But their effort was short lived. The breath would be taken from them. Their minds would wander... No one cut them off; we simply prayed - the Holy Spirit did the rest.

"The Spirit allows little human interference in the meetings, generally passing mistakes by unnoticed, or moving them out of the way Himself. Things that ordinarily we would feel must be corrected are often passed over, and a worse calamity averted thereby. To draw attention to them brings the spirit of fear on the saints, and they stop seeking.

"We were obliged to deal firmly with the extreme case, but in the main, the Spirit passed over and moved out of the way irregularities without further advertising them... Meetings must be controlled by way of the throne. A spiritual atmosphere must be created, through humility and prayer, that satan cannot live in."(*Another Wave Of Revival*, Frank Bartleman, p.60,61,77,90).

On one occasion Bartleman recalls that an opportunist jumped up during a lull in the meeting and presumably began to deliver a word from the Lord. He had only been going at it for about a minute when an old saint in the room stood up and simply asked, "Brother, what are you trying to do?" At which point he was totally shut down.

F. MOVE WITH GOD AND KEEP THE SHOVELS HANDY

Rather than throw out anything that resembles the prophetic because we have memories which make our spine crawl, let's become developed in our senses. Heb 5:14 *But strong meat belongeth to them that are of full age, even those who by reason of use have their senses exercised to discern both good and evil.*

The Body of Christ will have to deal with problems, perhaps on a regular basis seasonally, but the gifts of the Spirit are for our profit. 1 Cor 12:7 *But the manifestation of the Spirit is given to every man to profit withal.* Sometimes things can get messy but you have no ox to plow for the harvest if your stall is clean! Prov 14:4 *Where no oxen are, the crib is clean: but much increase is by the strength of the ox.* We just have to keep our shovels handy! I believe the components which make up our shovels are love, knowledge of the Word and wisdom.

III. REASON THREE: PAUL SAID SO

The third reason we need the prophetic is because PAUL SAID SO. Paul commands us to do just the opposite of despising prophesying. 1Thes 5:20 *Despise not prophesyings.* We are to actually encourage prophesying. Paul did - in four separate verses. 1 Cor *14:1 Follow after love; yet desire earnestly spiritual (gifts), but rather that ye may prophesy.* 1 Cor 14:5 *I would that ye all spake with tongues, but rather that ye prophesied: for greater is he that prophesieth than he that speaketh with tongues, except he interpret, that the church may receive edifying.* 1 Cor 14:31 *For ye may all prophesy one by one, that all may learn, and all may be comforted.* 1 Cor 14:39 *Wherefore, brethren, covet* [to be zealous in the pursuit of good, to be earnest - Thayer] *to prophesy, and forbid not to speak with tongues.*

A. THE WAY GOD SET THINGS UP

As far as prophets are concerned, Paul just simply tells us that that is the way God happened to set things up. In

God's Instruction Manual for the proper operation of the Body of Christ, prophets are given to us to help get us to God's goal for us. Eph 4:8 *Wherefore he saith, When he ascended up on high, he led captivity captive, and gave gifts unto men. 11 And he gave some, apostles; and some, prophets; and some, evangelists; and some, pastors and teachers; 12 For the perfecting of the saints, for the work of the ministry, for the edifying of the body of Christ: 13 TILL WE ALL COME in the unity of the faith, and of the knowledge of the Son of God, unto a perfect man, unto the measure of the stature of the fulness of Christ:*

The only manual that will give us the correct instructions and results is the Word of God. When we try to apply the manual of Personal Preference or the manual of "The Traditions Of Men" we will not be able to service or repair God's Product.

B. COMPLEMENTARY WISDOM OF GOD

The prophet is not more spiritual than the evangelist or the teacher. They are meant to complement one another. One has a facet of God's wisdom that the other does not. That is why we all need each other. Together we have the wisdom of God and together we have the Spirit without measure. Therefore, all of what God has given the church must function together in complementary unity.

IV. REASON FOUR: THE PROPHETIC CALLS US TO PERSEVERANCE SO WE CAN RECEIVE.

TO COUNTERACT PRESSURES AND DELAY

When God gives a promise He gives a witness of the Holy Spirit in our hearts. *He... put his Spirit in our hearts as a deposit, guaranteeing what is to come* (2Co 1:22). We allow pressures and delay to smother the witness, of the Holy Spirit, to promise. When we are on our way to the fulfillment of promise and the wind is not at our backs, the tendency is to turn around and go back so that we are not opposed by the wind. Rowing with the wind is much easier than rowing against the wind. But winds of opposition will come from the enemy because he does not want the promise of God to be fulfilled in us. If it is fulfilled in us it will not only revolutionize our lives but it will also bless those around us. It will advance the Kingdom of God.

Why then do we get discouraged or give up? The witness has not been removed. It is, however, that we are now looking at and listening to that which we perceive has interrupted or canceled promise.

B. TO REMIND US

There seems to exist some perverted rule which says, "That which bullies its way in gets to stay." Those defeating thoughts and doubts which demand to be considered begin to take the forefront and eventually replace the words and witness of promise. It is that prophetic gift which comes to remind us that God's Word holds the highest priority of consideration. We must ask ourselves, "What has priority? What is worthy of our focus? What will destroy promise? What will sustain promise? And which am I entertaining?"

We need the prophetic gift around regularly strengthening, encouraging and comforting (1Co 14:3) because the receiving of promise from God does not prevent waves from coming over the side of the boat. But the boat was already a considerable distance from land, buffeted by the waves because the wind was against it (Mt 14:24). The fact that we have received a prophecy does not guarantee that the wind will be at our backs. The waves coming over the side do not have to sink us. The wind does not have to destroy us. Believe it or not, those things do not even have to discourage us. They should actually build into us determination. They should make us more determined to focus on the goal.

C. BECAUSE AN ENEMY IS OPPOSING US

The prophetic reminds us that if the enemy is opposing us, he must be aware of the reality of our reaching promise, of walking in promise and doing him damage because of promise. Why would he oppose us if the fulfilling of promise would not cause him any damage? Why would he oppose us if there was little value in the promise or if there was little chance of it being fulfilled in us?

If you don't have a promise then get into the Word of God until one of the eight thousand begins to burn in your heart. In Lk.15 one son received what he asked for from his father. The other son, who griped about having nothing, was told that he would have already received if he would have only asked. If you never talk to your Father or spend time with Him, what do you think the result will be?

V. REASON FIVE: THE BOAT NEEDS STABILIZING
A. IN SPITE OF CIRCUMSTANCES

In Matthew, the disciples were terrified because they had no point of reference for what was happening. When the disciples saw him walking on the lake, they were terrified. "It's a ghost," they said, and cried out in fear (Mt 14:26). They did not see the circumstances allowing anyone, including Jesus, to walk on the water. They considered these circumstances as those that take you down and never let you up. These men of God had heard the heart-wrenching stories of fishermen suffering disaster at sea. Each of them could vividly tell a story of a relative or a friend who had not been able to attain the goal of "the other side." Nerve-testing reports of failure to "reach the other side" had settled upon their ears and they had used them as foundation stones to build a point of reference which, at this point, filled their hearts with terror..

Victory was not on their minds. There was absolutely no thought of nor any faith for victory over this situation. Perseverance was no more than an idealistic point made by preachers on land, in the safety of storm-free weather. They hunkered down and just got ready for anything this set of circumstances wanted to throw at them. That is not how you make it. That is not how you persevere. That is not how you receive the promise. The prophetic gift always, annoyingly refuses to let us simply "grab a root and grunt." Prophet Jesus immediately said to them: *"Take courage! It is I. Don't be afraid."* (v.27)

"It is I." It is Jesus who has given the promise and it is Jesus who will make good on it! Just look at who has given the promise. Jesus had far better transportation than a leaky old boat. The safest place on this occasion was not in the boat but on the water! Faith is for the purpose of getting out of the boat, not for asking Jesus to get into the boat.

His command is His guarantee. Immediately Jesus made the disciples get into the boat and go on ahead of him to the other side, while he dismissed the crowd. (Mt 14:22) The very command or promise of Jesus to do something is our guarantee that it can be done. Jesus told the disciples to go to the other side of the lake, which means that they would reach the other side of the lake. It does not mean that they would not encounter any opposition. It does not mean that they would simply sit down in the boat, put the oars in the water and a mere few moments later find themselves in safe harbor on the other side of the lake.

Jesus' command for them to go to the other side of the lake was their guarantee that they would get there. His involvement in the venture was their assurance that His help was available and ever-present. There was no concern on the part of Jesus that the newspaper might report a sad story the next day about a disaster befalling a radical religious group, e.g. "Religious Leader Gets Group Up Creek Without Paddle - Now Must Start Over - Looking For New Members And A Good Used Boat."

What God puts in the Son's hand is safe. However true that may be, when men start to walk in promise but find the wind and waves are against them, they turn their back to the wind and begin rowing in the opposite direction of promise. When waves come over the side of the boat and those inside lose heart or allow themselves to be distracted, others view the situation and say, "I don't blame them. The person who gave them that so-called encouragement should be stoned." There will always be someone who will sentimentally remind you that there is no need in your suffering hardship. Frail human sentiment will always be willing to offer, "If it's difficult, just do something different."

A prophecy is set down deep into an immovable foundation through a process called "endurance." *Take, my brethren, the prophets, who have spoken in the name of the Lord, for an example of suffering affliction, and of patience.* (Js 5:10) The prophets endured while their skulls were being split with stones and we tend to give up when 30 days have gone by and we aren't sitting on the porch of our cabin in the Promised Land. *Behold, we count them happy which endure. Ye have heard of the patience of Job, and have seen the end of the Lord; that the Lord is very pitiful, and of tender mercy.* (V.11) Endurance will bring us the end of the Lord. Cf. *For I know the thoughts that I think toward you, saith the Lord, thoughts of peace, and not of evil, to give you an expected end.* (Jer 29:11)

If there is anything the church needs today it is the determination to persevere. We live in a no-pain society that has taught us that we don't have to persevere. Men don't have to persevere through a prison sentence for heinous crimes against society. People don't have to persevere in education. They don't have to apply themselves to make a living. Some are simply handed an income.

Lack of perseverance is rewarded in an easy-way-out society. Greed in the upper echelon has taught people, low on the financial ladder, that those who have will get more and those who don't have will not have. We don't have to persevere for meals. Just pop one in the microwave and in a couple of minutes its ready. Restaurants advertise that your meal is free if you don't get it in five minutes. You don't have to persevere for things you want. Just fill out an application and while you pick out things which will wear out before you can pay the interest on them, your credit check will be done by computer in minutes.

If you don't want to persevere for promise, for purpose, for the Kingdom of God, there are churches on every corner and you will be able to find people who are disgruntled and disillusioned who will talk like you and tearfully hold your hand while they pray for the rapture in order to get out of this cruel old world that doesn't want Christians to prosper. But right in the face of so many condoning attitudes of forfeit and surrender and "legitimate excuses," the Word of God calls us to perseverance.

Peter saw Jesus. He wanted to be where Jesus was, doing what Jesus was doing. As long as Jesus was in it, it was possible. Peter said, "I want to come to you on the water." Jesus simply replied, "Come." Never at any point did Jesus withdraw permission or authority. Peter went down into the water because he focused on the circumstances. Jesus didn't leave or lose one ounce of power. He didn't change his mind about Peter walking on the water. Peter could have walked on the water to Jesus even if there had been a tornado. Wind and waves were already all about them before he ever stepped out of the boat. But he had his eyes on Jesus before he stepped out. Conditions do not have to be ideal for you to make it. The power of God to make it work has got to be present and we have got to keep our eyes on Him who calls us.

Peter could have made it all the way to Jesus. He was walking with nothing but a promise under his feet. He did not have to go down. Jesus wants us to be water-walkers. "Lord save me" is very acceptable communication between you and Jesus. You are going to make it all the way! You will make it with nothing but a promise under your feet.

Water is too thick to breathe but too thin to walk on. If you are going to make it, your trust and your measurement is not on the water. It is on the Master of the sea.

The Master of the Sea can command the sea to hold your weight or He can command it to part and form a wall on the right and on the left and let you pass! If you have to walk through the sea, know this: He has already walked through it ahead of you. According to Ps.77:19, God's footsteps were already in the bottom of the Red Sea although Israel did not see them! Water is not the substance that roadways are typically made of but it is possible to get to the other side when Jesus commands us go or come. Perseverance involves not taking our eyes off Jesus even though waves are splashing all around us(cf.Heb.12:1-3). Where is the answer when focusing on the waves and the wind?

WHO WOULD HAVE SAID?

God told Abram to begin calling himself Abraham ("Father of a multitude") ten years before he ever had a single child. It was God's calling and God's power that would get 100 year old Abraham to promise. Abraham's power, ability and resource could not cause his 90 year old wife to have a baby.

Not a single person on earth would have said Sarah would nurse children! *"Who would have said to Abraham that Sarah would nurse children? Yet I have borne him a son in his old age."* (Gen 21:7) Whose opinion has delayed the promise in your life? Whose opinion are you waiting for? The Word is enough! How many must say, "You are going to make it" before you believe it? No one has to say it. You have to say it. *For no matter how many promises God has made, they are "Yes" in Christ. And so through him the "Amen" is spoken by us to the glory of God.* (2Co.1:20). You are the one who says "Amen" to the promise.

Faith is the evidence of things not seen. Perseverance is the evidence of faith. Faith comes by hearing and hearing by the Word of God. The Word you are hearing today is stirring faith in you. Stand on that word. Use it to fight with. Say "Amen" to it. Sing it, say it or shout it while you are rowing the boat. The louder the opposing wind gets, the louder we profess the promises of God!

Faith is the evidence of things not seen. Perseverance is the evidence of faith. And praise is the evidence of perseverance. Praise says that the God who gave the promise is going to fulfill it. Praise says that no matter what the wind and waves look like, God is still able. Praise says that adversity and opposition cannot change the promises of God and cannot hinder His bringing them to pass. Problems don't change God. They prove God!

Chapter Ten
Decently And In Order

I. DECENTLY AND IN ORDER

1 Co.14:37-40 *If any man think himself to be a prophet, or spiritual, let him, acknowledge that the things that I write unto you are the commandments of the Lord. v38 But if any man be ignorant, let him be ignorant. v39 Wherefore, brethren, covet to prophesy, and forbid not to speak with tongues. v40 Let all things be done decently and in order.*

The word "decently" means *in a seemly manner, decently.* I'm not sure that Paul was trying to instruct us with a word that has the definition a modern mind would readily grab hold of. When Paul used the word, it doesn't necessarily refer to that which is *seemly or decent* to the Victorian mind of the nineteenth century or the mind of the twenty-first century which has been influenced by such Victorian preferences. Seeing that scripture interprets scripture, we need to take the whole of scripture for consideration. Examine some of Paul's statements about women. On one occasion he said, "Let women be quiet and ask their husbands at home. That type of thing leaves some thinking that a woman should not speak in church or instruct men. But yet at the same time he teaches that we all may prophesy. How is it possible for a woman to prophesy without speaking? We need to take the whole thing into consideration. So when we say *decently and in a seemly manner,* if someone wants to come along and say "decently and a seemly manner" is probably like the

Victorian mindset when everyone was "proper" and "quiet" and "in their place," we need to go back to Acts 2 and consider what happened there. According to Dr. Luke's account of that unprecedented event, there were 120 church people who were "drunk" in the Spirit with their hair on fire, speaking languages they had never spoken. Perhaps that is God's definition of *decently and in order*.

II. "DECENTLY AND IN ORDER" CAN INCLUDE NEW AND DIFFERENT THINGS

There are groups who are dismissing some very well-known churches from their ranks because they have determined that things are not being done "decently and in order" according to the manner in which they are interpreting Paul's demand for order. God is doing things lately that He has not done in a long time or that He has never done. Our Father is desirous to reveal more and more of Himself to us so that we might experience greater depths and heights in Him so that we might be more like Him and do more that is like Him. That would mean unprecedented experiences for us so that we could be taken to unprecedented levels for the purpose of glorifying His Name in unprecedented ways. Peter boldly stood up on the Day of Pentecost and proclaimed that the day's events were what Joel had predicted hundreds of years before (Joel 2:28-29). Yet, none of the day's activities, which we now picture in our minds when Pentecost is mentioned, were listed in Joel's prediction. Joel's prediction was actually quite mild compared to the Pentecostal exercises on that notable day.

Consider the well-documented events of the nineteenth century. All the great preachers who are highly esteemed by all Christian denominations, e.g. Finney and Wesley, wrote about the awesome demonstrations that were going on in their meetings. Their writings read like some of the writings describing recent moves of God. Seeing all the scriptural, historical and recent evidence, it should dawn on someone that, in prophetic ministry, God may be having us do some out-of-the-ordinary things. God is not into the extraordinary just for the sake of being extraordinary. But He brings those extraordinary experiences to us to reveal aspects of His Person to us. Anything we are not accustomed to, anything that we have not yet experienced, especially in God-proportions, is going to be extraordinary. The greatness of an awesome God can hardly be revealed through mundane, ordinary experiences.

If you have not seen Barbara Jimenez you are missing an opportunity to witness a unique ministry. She's a prophetess from New Orleans and she goes about the business of ministry in a most unique manner. Barbara ministered with Kathy and I in Houston on a Sunday morning. As we ministered at the end of the service, I asked Barbara, "Do you have a word for any of these people?" She joined us at the front and walked directly over to one particular young man who has acknowledged a call on his life He was standing there, decently and in order like a big city banker. Barbara walks up, forms her hand into something that you would see a karate expert do, and starts loudly saying "Da, da, da, da, da" while making motions with her hand all around the startled young man. Part of the time she is speaking in tongues and "breaking things off him" as she sees them in the Spirit and continues walking around and around him in the process. Kathy and I are accustomed to Barbara by now. I will be honest and tell you that I wasn't at first.

I was standing there watching her and praying and watching the young man to see if I was supposed to minister to him. Then, for some reason, I looked back at the congregation. About half of them were sitting there looking like raccoons looking at truck headlights, and I thought we were going to have a mass exodus. So I started explaining that this lady is doing what she sees in the Spirit because the scriptures teach us that God teaches our hands to war (2Sam 22:35). Although that did not completely soothe everyone's nerves, it seemed to help. Most are aware of the very things she is ministering to as she gestures. There have been a number of reports from those who have received such ministry who tell of deliverances from years of defeat and bondage in specific areas.

III. MORE THAT IS PROPHETIC, NOT LESS

It is very likely that we are going to be doing more prophetic movement and, as Barbara calls it, "prophetic gesturing" than we've seen heretofore. So, if we measure the reaction of the congregation that memorable morning, about fifty percent of them were concerned that we were suddenly indecent and out of order. Let us take caution lest we judge things to be out of order simply because they don't gel with our background or they don't make us feel comfortable because our preferences are pressing us to reject them. I think a good rule of thumb is, like Rodney Howard-Browne said: Don't say "That's not God," say "I don't understand it." And you'll be a whole lot better off. Some of the things I do now are things that used to be first on my list of things that God had nothing to do with.

IV. WE CAN WORK WITH THE ORDER

Order speaks of things being done in an arrangement; a due or right order, an orderly condition (Thayer). It should be understood that we need order. The Holy Spirit can work and anoint order, but it doesn't have to be the Victorian definition of order or any other antiquated prescription of order; however, it will be God's order that is in alignment with His Word and His purpose for a particular generation. Give God room so that the Holy Spirit sets the order. If you go to a place to minister and their definition of order is different than yours, you will go with the flow if you have come under the authority of that local house. So if they're a little wilder than you're used to you, may want to think twice before you go there or accept an invitation to minister there. And if they're a little more Victorian than your definition of decent and in order, you will need to go along with that too. If God is in the invitation for us to minister in a particular place, He is already aware of the restrictions or "liberties" of that gathering place and He most certainly realizes that we will have to adjust accordingly. A simple example is that there are places where I have to wear a tie. But by the time a preacher gets up to speak it's OK in Pentecostal/Charismatic services for a preacher to take off his tie. They just have to see that you have it on, then you can rip it off.

V. PROPHETIC TEMPERAMENT REQUIRES ORDER BE RECOGNIZED

The prophetic temperament especially requires the observance of order in the local assembly because the gifting is so vocal and can involve so much motion and energy. There is reason to believe that "Let everything be done decently and in order" was probably put in the Bible by the Holy Spirit because He knows the temperament of prophetically motivated people like we find listed in this section:

(1.) Prophetically gifted people tend to be like Boy Scouts — always prepared — whether local leadership or our "targets" of ministry are prepared for us or not. "Always prepared" does not mean that we force little old ladies to cross the street with us, like eager Boy Scouts have been humorously portrayed, or that we unleash what we are prepared to do on those who are not prepared to receive. At the Tomball Cowboy Church near Houston, I had a Boy Scout night. At the time they were meeting at Silverado Farms in the auction barn. There is a big auction arena that comes out from the wall, into the center of the room, where they can bring an animal out while it's being auctioned. At the end of the service that night Terry Thompson said to the people, "Bill Garrett and I are going to minister over here on this side and Marty and Shawn O'Hearn are going to minister on the other side. If you want prophetic ministry, get in one of these lines. In short time there were two long lines. We started ministering. Terry stands there like a Father and like a real decent human being and he speaks intelligently and he's able to communicate the heart of God to people. When I start prophesying I don't always look or sound just like him.

There was one cowboy that came up who had a couple of things in him that he didn't need in him and they started manifesting and he got a little loud and raucous. After him, a woman came up and began screaming. After a brief moment she fell down on her knees as the power of the Holy Spirit began to minister to her. Then suddenly, Terry's line got longer and mine got shorter. After a while, a lady walked up with a little boy in front of Terry and she said, "Is it OK if we switch lines. Is that alright? He said, "Yes, that's fine." The timid looking lady said, "I don't think he's ready for that other guy." And the little boy's eyes were as big as saucers. Not everybody is ready for all of us. If our yielding to their sense of order will help us strengthen, encourage and comfort them, we may have to suppress our opinions and serve them in the attitude of Jesus the Servant. Many times I get down on my knees, lower my voice and look small children in the eye to minister to them. If the Holy Spirit wasn't so loving and so versatile, He would not be able to draw the broad and diverse spectrum of humanity to the Father.

(2.) Sometimes prophetic people tend to be philosophical. "After all," they reason, "opportunity only knocks once. If I don't take this chance, I'll never get another one." So they jump up, even though its out of order; or they jump out there "when it hits them" cause they're stirred now and they want everybody else to be stirred. So, we can be philosophical, or perhaps pessimistic, that another opportunity will not ever come. Some folks might find that what they have to speak to someone will become more developed if they wait until a later opportunity. I saw some pastors at a meeting where I was not the primary speaker and the Lord gave me a vision concerning them while the speaker brought his message. I was anxious to speak to them of the vision and its application for their church. As the service went on I had other words for other people and never got to share it with them. I wondered if perhaps I should call when I got home but that didn't work out either. Two weeks later Kathy and I were in their church ministering on a Sunday morning. As the worship service was in progress, I had the vision again and the Lord spoke to my heart to call them up at the end of the message and give them the word then. The message just happened to be right in line with what the Lord wanted to say to the church through that vision. The lady and her husband told me afterwards that the word I had for them had answered a specific question she had asked the Lord just two days prior. Sometimes our sense of immediacy can hinder our Lord's timing if it is not checked.

(3.)   There are those prophetic people who are more musically inclined. They believe that "if you don't toot your own horn nobody else will." Even David didn't promote himself. Ps 78:71 *From following the ewes great with young he brought him to feed Jacob his people, and Israel his inheritance.* (KJV) God took David from a place of obscurity, where only a handful of sheep knew him, where he was not even respected among his brethren and made him a king. Sometimes people think that they must be seen in the "right place" with the "right people" or feel that they must keep trying until they are able to make that influential phone contact. Prophetic people are seen and heard more than average as it is. When they begin trying to promote themselves, they tend to appear pushy and obnoxious. If David had followed through with the temptation and urging he received to promote himself, God would have never allowed him to be king and he would have become guilty of touching God's anointed and displacing him before God was ready. (cf. 1Sam 24:4-5) Ps 75:6 *For promotion cometh neither from the east, nor from the west, nor from the south.* (KJV) 1 Chr 29:12 *Both riches and honour come of thee, and thou reignest over all; and in thine hand is power and might; and in thine hand it is to make great, and to give strength unto all.* (KJV) Ps 113:7-*He raiseth up the poor out of the dust, and lifteth the needy out of the dunghill; 8 That he may set him with princes, even with the princes of his people.* (KJV)

(4.) Some church leadership has used cautions like those given for handling guns. They always treat 'em like they're loaded. Some have cautioned us about "guns" warning us that they have a hair trigger — implying that they will go off at the most unexpected times. Using the warning that you don't aim a gun at anything unless you intend to shoot it, some pastors have not allowed "prophetic guns" to be aimed at any one in their church for fear that they will be fatally wounded. Not everything a prophetic person sees is supposed to be shared, especially in public or over a microphone. It could be that a large portion of what the Lord shows us is for intercession, especially if it is negative. Sometimes a vision or word we get is to be shared at a later time. There are times that a person is not ready to receive a word and it is possible that they would reject it and never consider it again. Just because a gun is loaded, doesn't mean that it has to be fired. There is a time to fire and a time to hold. God's timing enables us to hit the target accurately without leaving anyone fatally wounded.

(5.) Captains have always kept a constant watch for loose cannons. Captains of ships were always careful to keep their cannons tightly tied to the deck because a loose cannon could blow a hole in the ship and sink everyone with them. A "loose cannon" is someone who goes off at unexpected times putting ship and crew in danger. It is very difficult to get ahold of a cannon and get it tied down or committed anywhere. If a cannon got loose on the deck, especially under stormy conditions, it added to the tenseness of the circumstances and filled everyone aboard with apprehension, not knowing when it might go off and not knowing how much damage might be done. On occasion, one has broken loose and fallen overboard. Many pastors and churches fear prophetic people because they have known one or two that could not be tied to any authority. They would get loose from their authority that gave them oversight and kept them in check and then they would do and say things that caused damage. Others have gotten loose from firm foundations and carelessly rolled about the "deck" threatening to do damage with their loose revelations and teachings. We should practice caution that we do not get caught up in trying to get in on prophesying the latest thing that the big names are prophesying. Trying to find a "handle" we can grab and identify with on the latest subject could leave us rolling about a "pitching deck" that might cause damage to the local vessel. Teachers and pastors need the Word and the Holy Spirit and the counsel of many but prophetic people tend to get on the ethereal edge more often, so we really need those firm anchors to hold us on the true mark. Cf. Prov 12:15 *The way of a fool is right in his own eyes, but a wise man is he who listens to counsel.* (NAS) Prov 19:20 *Listen to counsel and accept discipline, that you may be wise the rest of your days.* (NAS) Prov 11:14 *Where there is no guidance, the people fall, but in abundance of counselors there is victory.* (NAS)

VI. LOCAL DEFINITION

I think a good rule of thumb to define "decently and in order" is to say that it is whatever the local house allows. "Decently and in order," as defined by local authority, takes a big load off of me. There is one church that has announced that I was going to be there the following Sunday morning and half of them did not come but stayed home. I went into a church where the elders had decided to dismiss the pastor. They were going to take a vote. That church was not supposedly set up for voting. It was set up under an eldership with an apostle. In the past, the spiritual leaders of that church had made those decisions in the fear of the Lord without a democratic consensus from everyone else. I got a phone call on Saturday night about what was coming down the next Sunday morning. I walked in there and at the first opportunity I got up and took the microphone and began to read them the riot act. I thought I was going to get hit in the mouth afterwards. An elder took me back in to the pastor's office. He was so angry, I thought he was going to have a heart attack. He called me stupid, he called me a false prophet, he called me names I don't want to repeat right now. God told me to sit back in that beautiful wing-back chair in that pastor's office in that big fancy church and not say a word. That was one of the most difficult things I have ever done in my life. I sat back, shut my mouth and in two or three minutes that angry elder was a babbling and so confused, he forgot what he was trying to say. He wasn't making sense and he'd shake his head and he would stop and start over.

If we give it an opportunity, "decently and in order" will take a load off of us. If I would have been willing to realize before I went there that there was already a sense of "decency and in order" in that local house, I might could have done more good than I did damage with those elders. Local leadership, the set-in man, the set-in woman, whoever is the local set-in leader there bears the responsibility and persons who submit to that are relieved of much burden. Furthermore, the apostle who happens to be in charge of a particular meeting or mission, bears the responsibility of ministry by those who are under their direction. If you go with an apostle or someone on a mission to Central America or Europe or even to small-town America to minister with them, you must be submitted to their sense of order. Just because there is a prophetic zealousness rising up in you (and I can tell you stories that would make your hair stand on end) you never want to get out of the order of the people you are with and whose authority you are under. When they have given certain guidelines and they cut you off or they stop you or they hold you within very limited perimeters, all you have to be is frustrated. You don't have to try to override any of that because they have just taken the responsibility off of your shoulders. They must answer to those who have asked them to come and minister. They answer for their actions and the actions of those they have invited with them on the mission. They will also answer to God.

It doesn't matter what we're seeing or how clearly we're seeing it. If those who are over us and are responsible for us are putting certain restrictions on us and limitations, we yield to that. Yield to that manner of "decency and order" and God will cause them to bear the responsibility for it and it will be seen that you are willing to honor God's positioning of another. It's possible that they see something or know something about the situation that we don't. There have been times I felt I had a word on a matter but the apostle I was with asked me to hold it because he knew something about someone in the situation that would require this being dealt with in private. Boy, was I glad my zealousness didn't load my mouth and override my sense of proper order! I discovered later that disaster was averted because I had enough sense (at least at that one time) to yield to the authority that I was with. It's a beautiful thing to travel some place else with another authority. I believe that's why, several times, the Bible lists apostles and prophets together. So, what is considered to be "decency and in order" will vary from place to place. Flow with it. It is best to yield to those set in authority or that authority person you're with. I wish somebody would have taught me this in the early years when I first discovered there was a prophetic gift in me so that I might have been spared several embarrassing and door-closing scenarios. God has an order that will bring the desired results. Sometimes we just have to make sure that we stay in relationship long enough to find out what that order is.

Chapter Eleven
Gifts, Titles And Callings

I. YOUR GIFT MAKES A PLACE

Your gift will make a place for you in the Body of Christ (cf Prov 18:16). You don't have to strain at it nor do you have to make a place for yourself. Allow God to develop in you the particular gifting the Holy Spirit has put in you. The typical scriptural scenario will show that it takes time to develop the Spirit's gifts in humans.

One place the church makes mistakes concerning its effectiveness is when we assume that appointing or voting a person to a position or title means that they will be able to effectively function there. Placing labels and badges on people doesn't make them what the label calls them.

II. THE GIFT WILL FIND SOME FORM OF EXPRESSION

If a person is a teacher, it seems like they are constantly about the business of teaching someone something, whether standing behind a podium or at a restaurant or on the golf course. If a person is a pastor, their lifestyle will exhibit concern for the Lord's sheep. They will be concerned over people's needs and be about the business of counseling and watching over persons.

We should be very cautious about giving people titles when we need positions filled or giftings expressed in the local body. Titles are much easier to give than they are to take away. If someone in our church is an elder, we will recognize it when we see them pastoring people. When we notice people looking to them for counsel and pastoral ministry we can then lay hands on them and say "Amen" to what God has obviously already done.

Where prophetic gifting is concerned, the circumstances are a little different. Some begin calling themselves a prophet after they have gained a reputation for prophesying. I remember situations where a person who prophesied regularly was called a prophet by observers and it caused that person a great deal of frustration because their motivational gift was evangelist or pastor. Just because someone prophesies does not mean they are a prophet, no matter how often they prophesy.

III. THREE CATEGORIES

There are three categories concerning prophetic gifting which we need to consider. These categories are: (1.) the Spirit of prophecy, (2.) the gift of prophecy and (3.) the office of prophet.

(1.) The Spirit of Prophecy.

When a group of people are gathered and the Holy Spirit begins to move upon them, any believer in the group may be enabled to prophesy (cf. 1Co 14:24,31; Rev 19:10). People who have never prophesied before or perhaps people who prophesy rarely can prophesy when the Spirit of prophecy moves upon the group.

(2.) The Gift of Prophecy.

God uses persons in the gift of prophecy so that they may minister at any time such edification is desired by Him (cf

1Co 12:11). These persons can prophesy even when the Spirit of prophecy is not resting upon the congregation. I minister from time to time with persons who have the gift of prophecy and they do as much prophesying as most prophets.

3.) The Office of Prophet (Some refer to this as the Ministry Gift of Prophet)

Those operating in the gift of prophecy (or those operating under the Spirit of prophecy) will fulfill 1Co 14:3 "strengthen, encourage, comfort" (NIV). While "strengthen, encourage and comfort" are part of the prophetic office, prophets have yet other responsibilities incumbent upon them. The prophetic office carries with it a level of authority not found in the other two categories. Prophets also minister in the laying on of hands and identifying of giftings in persons (cf 1Tim 1:18). They also speak correction under the oversight of local leadership. Prediction is also an element of the prophet's ministry and it is regularly a part of his or her prophecies (cf Acts 11:27-28; 21:10-11).

IV. THE CALL IS ONLY THE BEGINNING - NOW DEVELOPMENT

When a person receives a call to prophetic ministry, he or she must understand that the call is only the beginning. One does not simply step into a realm of authority and begin a powerful prophetic ministry. God first **(1.)** puts the **awareness of a call** in a person. Secondly, **(2.)** He begins to give **confirmation** to that call through others (cf. Rom 12:3-5) while thirdly, **(3.)** He d**evelops a hearing ear** in the person who has received the call. God may take many years to develop a hearing ear in a person. Samuel didn't order 1,000 ministry cards the day after he heard God's voice in the night. (Cf. 1Sam 2:21 *"and the boy Samuel grew before the Lord";* 26 *Now the boy Samuel was growing in stature and in favor both with the LORD and with men.* (NAS); 1 Sam 3:19 *Thus Samuel grew and the LORD was with him and let none of his words fail.* (NAS) Adam Clarke: **"Samuel grew" means "increased to manhood."**

DEVELOPMENT AND CONFIRMATION: 1Sam 3:20 *And all Israel from Dan even to Beersheba knew that Samuel was confirmed as a prophet of the LORD.* (NAS)

As God develops the hearing ear, He is also working on the person's character. ....*Them that honor me, I will honor....* (1Sam 2:30). Those who "honor God" are those who yield to His process of development and time. The developing of the person's character includes God getting a hold on his or her tongue. Since we have been accustomed to speaking from our own personal reference point, **God must begin to change our reference point to His reference point. People, circumstances and time** will be used by God to mold us and shape us and transform us into a usable vessel. *Education is generally defined that series of means by which the human understanding is* **gradually enlightened**, *and the dispositions of the heart are* **(1.)** *corrected,* **(2.)** *formed, and* **(3.)** *brought forth* (Adam Clarke).

God will take us through stages to develop in us a hearing ear and an obedient tongue. God is so faithful to His plan that He will not omit any of the stages of development. Sometimes each stage takes a different amount of time in one person as compared to another but He is faithful to take each of us through each stage until He has useful vessels.

V. PERSONAL TESTIMONY

As a child, I sensed a call of God upon my life. At 16 years of age, I received a call to preach when responding to an altar call at youth camp. For the next seven years I traveled as an evangelist. The first time I ever received a prophecy was when I was 18. Not having knowledge of the prophetic gifts, I didn't understand that it was a prophecy but it greatly affected my life. Though I have seen numerous prophecies fulfilled, I have not yet seen that one fulfilled.

After traveling for seven years as an evangelist, I was an associate pastor for four and a half years. One time in a meeting I saw someone prophesy to a person and something welled up within me and I knew that was what I wanted to do... what I must do. Still nothing was happening along those lines.

Between the time of serving as an associate and pastoring for two years, I worked in a paint and body shop. Then after pastoring (or trying to), it was back to the paint and body shop for four more years! God was really taking me through some stages during that time. All through the decade of the eighties I went from the heat of the crucible to the molding of the potter's wheel to the chisel and hammer of the sculptor. I most certainly haven't arrived but at least the heat of the crucible isn't as intense, thank God.

In 1990 I attended a conference with Warren Piersol where Leon Price was one of the presbyters. Brother Leon laid his hands on me and prophesied that the prophetic word was in me and confirmed what Brother Warren had already seen. Ron Wood was serving in the presbytery and confirmed the word. That was on a Friday. In service on Sunday I was prophesying to anything that moved and if it didn't move, I kicked it just to make sure.

The following week Trinity Life Church in Conroe held a prophetic conference and Warren Piersol was one of the speakers. Brother Warren had told the pastor (Terry Thompson) about the prophecy I had received. When it was discovered that more persons were needed to help prophesy, Terry called me up to help. I was scared spitless! I couldn't even swallow. But when Bill Garrett and others began to prophesy, it began to stir that anointing in me and I began to prophesy also.

The last night of the conference was a Sunday night. Brother Warren was speaking that night. When He finished speaking he told the congregation that the Lord used me to prophesy and that if anyone had not received a prophecy during the conference, that I would prophesy to them if they would just come forward and line up. There were probably 100 people who came forward that night. I was sweating bricks! But when I opened my mouth, God filled it. Doug Roberts had prophesied to me that I would never run out of words to give because God was the one who filled the "seed bag" with words. For the last eleven years God has most certainly fulfilled that prophecy.

Although I prophesy regularly and have prophesied to over 5,000 people, God is still taking me through stages of development. There have been times when several hundred people were witnesses to my being corrected by God. Then there have been times when God has allowed me to learn very valuable lessons from the "cheap seats," that is, I have been able to receive correction and adjustments to my attitude with only one or two people around.

A very valuable lesson God has brought to me is that we "have this treasure in earthen vessels" (2Co 4:7). It has taught me to be able to release the gift that is in me and also to receive wonderful gifts in others even though they don't necessarily fit the category of "persons I would most prefer to receive from."

In the mid-eighties I was pastoring in the Houston area. One of our home groups was meeting in an elder's home. I was covered from head to toe with poison ivy and was very, very miserable. I was wearing a long-sleeve shirt trying to hide the spreading menace. No one was aware that I had this allergic reaction.

After a time of worship and prayer, a twelve year old boy walked up and asked if he could pray for me. He told me that he had a gift of healing for me. I thought that the gesture was very cute and since his dad was an elder, it wouldn't hurt to let this little child pray for me.

The moment he put his small hand on my itching chest, fire and lightning shot from my head to my toes and the itching immediately stopped. Within two days the rash had completely disappeared!

If we can get beyond the way a person postures themselves or the way they dress or comb their hair or how loud they are or what age or sex they are, we can receive what God has put in them for us. We don't have to be completely in awe of a person to receive some good gift from an individual.

VI. SIMPLY RELEASE THE GIFT OF GOD

Once I realized that it is the gift of God that I was to release to people, a great deal of the difficulty and self-awareness disappeared. *"For I long to see you, that I may impart to you some spiritual gift, to the end ye may be established;"* (Rom 1:11). The **gifts of the Spirit are just that. They are the gifts OF THE SPIRIT.** If I am a prophetic minister, the prophetic gift is not mine. It's for that person whom the Spirit wants to give that gift. As a minister, all I do is release the gift that is in me.

VII. NOT FORCED OR WORKED UP

That is the simplicity of ministry or calling or gifting. The minister does not have to work up a certain feeling or atmosphere. The minister does not have to make a place for himself or force himself on anyone. There are people who need to receive ministry and there are people God wants to minister through (1Co 12:4-11).

God will **mold** and **chip away** and **apply the heat** over the course of many months and many years. His purpose is not to get us to heaven but to mold us into the image of Christ. That is why we will have apostles, prophets, evangelists, pastors and teachers. He is using each one *for the perfecting of the saints, for the work of the ministry, for the edifying of the Body of Christ: Till we all come.... unto the measure of the stature of the fullness of Christ.* (Eph 4)

Chapter Twelve

Now That I Have Received a Prophecy

Receiving a prophecy does not mean that you have just received an all-expense-paid ride on a magic carpet. Prophecies are conditional upon (1.) our **faith** in receiving them, (2.) our **obedience** to God and (3.) our **endurance** through the preparation period with a "moldable attitude."

Being given a prophecy is like being given a suit of clothes that we have to grow into. God gives us a word of prophecy to make our potential obvious to us. That is, the prophecy is the way God sees us. We may not be the spiritual person or the person of faith that the prophecy describes but our **faith, obedience and endurance** We will grow to the suit of clothes God gives us.

God prophesied through His prophet that He was going to give a certain land to His people Israel. Whenever they did not simply march out of Egypt and into the "promised land," they were very discouraged and were ready to return to the captivity and slavery of Egypt. It seems they understood (or preferred to understand) that they would simply be whisked away to the fulfillment of the prophecy on some type of "magic carpet" and be landed in the middle of that land in full, unquestioned possession of it.

One lesson which we may learn free of charge is that God's promises and prophecies are not an anesthetic which dull our feelings and emotions until the "magic carpet" lands in the desired time and location. I have talked to people whom I have prophesied over. Some of them have been very disappointed after six months or a year that their prophecy has not come to pass. Where I begin to ask questions is at the points of (1.) **faith**, (2.) **obedience** and (3.) **endurance**. **Faith** will cause us to **act** on the Word of God. **Obedience** will cause us to be **true** to the Word of God rather than giving in to our emotions and disappointments. **Endurance** is just a lot of **work** and there is nothing at all easy about that.

*"Behold, the Lord thy God hath set the land before thee: **go up and possess it**, as the Lord God of thy fathers hath said unto thee; **fear not, neither be discouraged.***

*And they took the fruit of the land in their hands, and brought it down unto us, and brought us word again, and said, **It is a good land which the Lord our God doth give us.***" (Deut 1:21,25 KJV)

The great news is that the promise or the prophecy which God is giving us is *"a good land."* That is why satan fights you so hard over your prophecy. It is a "good land" and it is worth having. The problem satan has with it is he knows that the fulfillment of it will do damage to him and his purpose. He knows that when you embrace that prophecy and begin to walk in it, you will displace his claims on lives and take territory for the Kingdom of God.

OK, that sounds great but how do I "embrace the promise?" How do I "take the land?" According to the example in the book of Deuteronomy, Israel took the land by dispossessing the enemy. Discouragement, fear of failure or rejection and doubts of others are all enemies of promise. Displace those enemies with TRUTH.

Always stand on the Word of God. The house that is built on the Rock (Truth) is able to withstand the storm (Mt 7:24). The house that is built on the sand (emotions, fears, doubts) will fall. Displace the enemies of promise with the words out of your own mouth. *Let us hold unswervingly to the hope which we profess* (Heb 10:23 NIV). If I understand the scriptural concept here, it is useless to hold to hopes which we do not profess with our mouths.

"And thou shalt do that which is right and good in the sight of the Lord: that it may be well with thee, and that thou mayest go in and possess the good land which the Lord sware unto thy fathers," (Deut 6:18) If we obey God and do right, it will *"go well"* with us. We will come into the land in God's timing. God will not bring us into the fulfillment of prophecy prematurely. He will grow us into the "suit" so that we will fit into it properly.

Another aspect of consideration, after having received a prophecy, is the matter of your prophecy being judged. The principle is found in 1Co 14:29. *Let the prophets speak two or three, and let the other judge.*(KJV) We have the Scriptures as the inspired, inerrant Word of God. Prophecy in the New Testament era should be judged.

There was one pastor who told me he was not going to have me come minister at his church any more. When I asked him why he told me that I created too much work for him. Wherever I minister I urge pastors and their people to judge the prophecies that I give. One church where I ministered had everyone's prophecy typed out. After that, the pastor and elders met with each individual and went over their prophecy with them. Misunderstandings were given answers and the Lord even enabled those spiritual leaders to help interpret the picturesque language which some of the prophecies contained. There were even two couples who rejected their prophecies completely believing that they were not the word of the Lord to them.

God has given us pastors and elders for a "covering" to teach us, counsel us and to watch for our souls. There should always be apostles and pastors and spiritual leaders to whom prophets are accountable. These leaders may be appealed to if the prophecy or the prophet are questionable.

I require that all prophecies be spoken over a microphone and recorded so that they may be judged by spiritual leadership. There is even a need to beware of some who give so-called "parking lot prophecies." It seems that there is always someone around who loves to pull persons over to the side and whisper in their ear.

Recently I heard a story about an angry, disgruntled preacher who was visiting a church not in his city. He told a young boy to go to a woman he saw across the congregation and tell her that she had 40 demons. The woman jumped up and ran out hysterical. She was devastated. The young boy burst into tears and never wanted to be seen in public again. Her best response would have been to proclaim aloud, "I don't receive that!" and then secondly, to report him to local leadership A.S.A.P.!

Prophetic ministry has a bad name in some places and it is certainly no wonder. The New Testament concept of accountability is a sound safety measure for both the one receiving prophecy and the one prophesying.

If your pastor has taught you to go to your designated elder for ministry and counsel, then take your prophecy to him or her and the two of you pray over it. If you have been taught to take things directly to your pastor, then make an appointment with that person and prayerfully judge your prophecy.

If you and the person who has spiritual oversight for your life have received a witness of the Holy Spirit, then diligently "take the good land." If it was prophesied that you are a teacher then begin preparation to teach. Don't expect the pastor to turn the pulpit over to you next Sunday. After a season of preparation and growth, God will begin opening doors.

If you truly are a teacher or a prophet or an apostle or an evangelist or a pastor, that anointing will work in you in such a way that others in the Body of Christ will begin to recognize it. Just because a person has received a prophecy, no matter how grand and great, it does not mean that they can go about things as they see fit.

The best thing a person can do is to submit themselves to spiritual authority. Seek guidance and counsel concerning your gifting. Apostles and pastors have been given to us to prepare us for the work of the ministry. They are the "fathering ministries" which will, with the other five-fold, bring us *"unto the measure of the stature of the fulness of Christ."* (Eph 4:13-KJV)

Chapter Thirteen

Now That I Have Begun to Prophesy

The Spirit of the Lord is being poured out upon all flesh just as Joel has prophesied. Many people in local congregations and our sons and daughters are prophesying. With the prophetic move of God, which has been sweeping the globe over the last couple of decades, we have been striving to equip the saints for the work of the ministry. There are sound principles which we must adhere to in order to effectively do "the work of the ministry." This article will deal with some of those principles which may be applied, especially for those who prophesy. We will consider principles in the areas of (1.) the gift of prophecy; (2.) operating in the gift of prophecy; (3.) guidelines for prophesying; and (4.) the personal life of the person who prophesies. This would be a good article for pastors to duplicate and pass to persons in their congregation who "covet to prophesy."

(1.) THE GIFT

One of the most amazing things about living in this age is that we get to speak Father's heart to other people. I have heard it said that Old Testament prophecy is revelation received and that New Testament prophecy is revelation perceived. He allows us to express the impressions, visions and thoughts which He gives us. We are allowed to express them through our personality and in our own words. What grace this is!

An important factor which seems to be seldom considered is the fact that not all who prophesy are prophets. Pastors frequently share with me stories about persons who walk into their church and announce that they are a prophet. Immediately "lights and warning bells go off" and those persons find themselves not so warmly received. Many pastors have had harrowing experiences with persons who seem determined to "push" themselves and their "gift," if in fact they actually do have a gift. These type scenarios are probably the result of our not taking the time to teach folks that, if indeed there is a gift, the Body of Christ will recognize it and embrace it. Relationship defines. If a person has relationship with the Body of Christ that relationship will define who and what they are. A person who pushes themselves or their gift is setting themselves up for an improper display of the gift and setting themselves up for rejection. The person who pushes could likely close the door to prophetic ministry in that church.

Even if a person truly is a prophet that does not mean he/she will be received as one everywhere he/she goes. In scripture Paul writes that he realized he was not accepted by all as an apostle (1Co 9:2). He also speaks of not trying to go beyond the measure or boundary that God had set for him (2Co 10:13-15).

Those operating in the gift of prophecy, or those operating under the Spirit of prophecy, will fulfill 1Co 14:3 "strengthen, encourage, comfort" (NIV). While "strengthen, encourage and comfort" are part of the prophetic office, prophets have yet other responsibilities incumbent upon them. The prophetic office carries with it a level of authority not found in the other two categories.

Prophets also minister in the laying on of hands and identifying of giftings in persons (cf 1Tim 1:18). They also speak correction under the oversight of local leadership. Prediction is also an element of the prophet's ministry and it is regularly a part of his or her prophecies (cf Acts 11:27-28; 21:10-11).

"To possess the office of a prophet, one requires a sovereign calling, extensive training, and multiple encounters with the presence of God. Unlike the other levels of the prophetic, the prophet operates in a governmental office, directing and correcting the Church. He lives in a realm of forth-telling, rebuke, affirmation, revelation, illumination, prophetic utterance, prediction, encouragement, dreams, visions, correction and ministry confirmation (Larry Randolph, User Friendly Prophecy)."

"The office of a prophet not only ministers in edification, exhortation, and comfort, but also operates in the realm of guidance, rebuke, judgment, correction, and revelation. The one who has the gift of prophecy but is not a prophet does not function in any of these latter realms. The prophetic office brings a realm of spiritual authority into the prophetic ministry not found in the other two realms of prophetic function (David Blomgren, Prophetic Gatherings In The Church)."

Someone called to serve the Body of Christ in the office of prophet does not simply step into all of the authority listed above just because they have received a call. Father invests much time, training and circumstantial preparation in a person before He is able to trust them with such responsibility. Most who are presently attempting to function in that office are most likely "prophets in training."

Probably the great majority of those who prophesy

are not prophets. Those operating in the gift of prophecy or the Spirit of prophecy will find their parameters laid out for them in 1Co 14:3. *"But everyone who prophesies speaks to men for their strengthening, encouragement and comfort."*(NIV) There is often a tendency in prophetic people to lean toward harshness or being judgmental. The best rule of thumb is to refrain from being judgmental and STRENGTHEN, ENCOURAGE AND COMFORT. The more a person speaks, the more that person is accountable for.... before God and man.

(2.) OPERATING IN THE GIFT

Prophesying is spontaneously speaking forth that which our amazing God has put upon our heart and stirred within our spirit. He is desiring to encourage and show His intent for the potential He has put in His precious one that we are prophesying to. In a display of "heaven kissing earth," a person who prophesies has the privilege of being caught in the middle of that divine expression. In that edifying position, it is possible for one to put too much of one's self into the mix, thereby distorting the intended message. When we are emotionally moved in someone's behalf, it is possible to add in a "little something" that we wish for that person - which also distorts the message.

It is also possible for one to withhold a portion of the message. One may not intentionally set out to withhold a single thing in ministry but because of the "look" of the person we are speaking to, we may feel that this particular word does not "fit" them. There may also be the possibility that what we are "hearing" is such a grand sounding word that we feel it would sound unfit or even foolish to say such a thing to this person. I continually pray, "Father, help me not to say one word more or one word less than you want said."

He who prophesies takes a risk each and every time he prophesies. That is the faith element. There is the risk that one will be rejected in attempting to edify through the prophetic gift. The risk also exists in that one could possibly "miss it." Everyone who has ever prophesied has "missed it" at one time or other. One does not become a zombie or a thoughtless puppet just because the Holy Spirit has moved upon them to prophesy. Perhaps that would be one good reason to require all prophecies be given over a mic and recorded. Such prior knowledge may help us haughty humans to keep ourselves in check.

Chapter Fourteen
Keys Toward Prophesying And Ministry

I. TENDING TO BUSINESS

Notice the title here. The word "toward" has much purpose in it. In other words, there are things that we need to tend to before we go about the business of prophesying. There was a time a couple of decades ago when the prophetic began to be restored to the Body of Christ. People began to be moved upon by the Spirit of prophecy or began to operate in a gift of prophecy or began to walk in the office of a prophet. When all of that began happening, people were really zealous and many of us were just doing it without knowing anything about it or taking any time to learn anything about it.

About a half-century ago teachers were beginning to get revelation about who we are in Christ Jesus and that we have authority in that position. But very few were attempting to discover anything about that authority and its implications and responsibilities. As a result, in some cases, there were people who like the sons of Sceva were going out on their own and, as it were, "running out of houses naked" because of a lack of knowledge about gifts, authority, responsibility and relationship in the Kingdom of God.

One lady we know told us an interesting story when she took it on herself to do deliverance at a mental hospital. She had heard about the brother of an acquaintance who was in lock-up due to his mental problems. She decided that she would go and deliver him of the demon that was behind all those interesting reports. This dear zealous person had heard some wonderful stories from the Charismatics she was fellowshipping of exercising the power and authority of the believer but she hadn't heard biblical principles on the matter.

The doctor's aide brought the man to the meeting room and sat him across the table from this lady and told her she had ten minutes visitation time as he was on his way out the door. She began to command the devil to come out of him in the Name of Jesus. The man began to manifest, his face contorted and he began to growl. It was not quite the scenario she had anticipated from the pieced-together reports of her friends' victorious encounters. Not really knowing what to do next she began to cry out, "Get back in, in the Name of Jesus!" and she reported with much relief that, in fact, the demon went back in.

II. AUTHORITY AND RESPONSIBILITY

In many cases we were just told that we had authority and that we could do stuff with it. We didn't know how to use it nor did we know how to stay under the authority of God, under the authority of spiritual oversight and responsibly act in that authority. Nothing was ever discussed about finding out what our "measure of rule" was (cf.2Co 10:12-18). It really is wise for us to back up, even though it may mean having to restrain "faith-backed" zeal, and learn some foundations that are firm ground to stand on, especially when things tend to get shaky. In some cases we're trying to take two or three steps forward and we're finding out that we're having to back up one or two and say, "Excuse us Father, we forgot about Hosea 4:6": *My people are destroyed for lack of knowledge* (NAS). There is a tendency to forget about the whole counsel of God (cf.Acts 20:27; Isa 46:10-11; Jer 23:22; Mt 28:20). Here is an area where it became visible through the '80's that prophetic people truly do need that complementary gift of teacher. We have stopped short when we just take the parts that excite us at the time. Now, as a result, we are having to actually back up and get some of the elemental things taken care of and understood so we can go on. Those Kingdom opportunities and potential that await us in the days to come require we be prepared to act effectively, efficiently and excellently if we are to speak or act at all in the Name of our Lord.

III. FATHER'S KEYS AND FATHER'S SONS

God is not going to give the keys of a brand new Lexus to a three-year-old. Three-year-olds ride tricycles and stick horses. Sons (cf.Heb 2:10; Rom 8:14) have a desire for the Three E's of ministry: Efficiency, Effectiveness and Excellence. *Whoever speaks, {let him speak,} as it were, the utterances of God; whoever serves, {let him do so} as by the strength which God supplies; so that in all things God may be glorified through Jesus Christ, to whom belongs the glory and dominion forever and ever. Amen.* (1Pe 4:11, NAS; also Ps 9:1; 1Co 10:31). Those are elements in the makeup of the key to "the Lexus" of the privilege and responsibility Father wants His sons to experience. But some folks are like leftover hippies from the 60's who are willing to drive a rusted-out Volkswagen. However, our Father is looking for mature sons that can be relied upon to operate in the vehicle of His authority and carry the opportunities of manhood. Gal 4:5 ....*to redeem those under law,* ***that we might receive the full rights of*** *sons*. (NIV)

A mature son is one who has been afforded the right of acting in his father's name as well as having the portion of his father's land, etc., which is properly his according to heirship. The many-colored coat of Joseph was representative of authority. His older brothers deeply resented the fact that their father had favored him with his authority and openly showed it by placing a visible sign upon his person. I'm not speaking here of so-called prosperity concepts but of privilege to operate in the power of the Holy Spirit by grace provided us through an awesomely powerful resurrected Jesus. The principle of a father desiring to release his authority upon his son (and power to act in his name) is a repeated theme in the Bible. ("sons" in scripture is not a term referring to gender but to position and "manhood" represents maturity, not maleness; also Lk 15:22; Jn 1:12; Gal 3:26-4:7; Heb 2:10)

IV. GREAT AND MIGHTY THINGS THOU KNOWEST NOT

Almighty God is interested in using His sons in the "high-powered thing" in this hour. I believe scripture demonstrates for us that there is a "high-powered thing" that is above and beyond (and on a totally different level and category from) anything that we have ever comprehended or understood in God. When hunters go after big game, they take a "high-powered" rifle to properly do the job. My Dad once told me about a man in a difficult legal jam who got himself a "high-powered" lawyer to get him out. Jer 33:3 *Call unto me, and I will answer thee, and shew thee great and mighty things, which thou knowest not.* (KJV) Cf. Micah 7:15: Eph 3:20; Isa 45:3. The high level of opposition we are up against in this world requires a high level of power in response. The Father must know that He can expect us to obey in any given situation. Such a trust on His part would be witness to the fact that our sentiments and our emotions are fully in check -- that our *meat is to do the will of him that sent me, and to finish his work.* (Jn 4:34, KJV) We desire to speak for God but our tongue must be submitted to His control and out from under the control of our emotions and prejudices.

These are some reasons why, often, God has not been able to release "thy Kingdom come" power and authority to those who, in prayer, most zealously seek Him for it. It is because of our lack of knowledge -- that understanding of the Father/son relationship that is totally trusting on both sides. A child has a great zealousness to get his hands on machinery and hear the sounds and feel the momentum and experience the power. Put him behind the wheel of that Lexus and see how long that Lexus lasts -- and then throw in a little imagination concerning property damage and the bruising effects on life and limb of those who happen to be around when he is trying to manipulate that vehicle. Well, God's vehicle of power was made possible by the blood of Jesus so we're talking about a whole new category. There are people who place high hopes on Acts 17:30 and have their fingers crossed that God still winks at ignorance. God quit winking.

V. UNDER AUTHORITY.... THEN.... IN AUTHORITY

We've got to be men and women *under authority* before we can be men and women *in authority*. Loosey--goosey morals and mushy lines of accountability will not meet the standards of a Holy God. There are those who are willing to simply overlook every kind of moral and ethical "fall" while patting such persons on the back and acting as though they did nothing more than burp in public. Some persons have not even been required to walk out any season of repentance but simply go on about their business with somewhat of an embarrassed posture when scriptural standard requires *that they should repent and turn to God, performing deeds appropriate to repentance.* (Acts 26:20, NAS)

God does not continually release His authority to those who decide varying standards for various individuals according to their position or notoriety. Sons are those who operate upon the standards of God's Word and God's character — for themselves and others. We do not get to make decisions of authority until we are submitted to authority and stay within its parameters. That doesn't mean that those who use elastic theology, when convenient, won't have successful organizations. Crowd-building methodology and money-raising tactics work in any field of endeavor. Where we will see the difference is in the area of spiritual power to do the works of Jesus.

Acts 2:22 *"Men of Israel, listen to these words: Jesus the Nazarene, a man attested to you by God with miracles and wonders and signs which God performed through Him in your midst, just as you yourselves know--*(NAS)

Rom 14:17 *for the kingdom of God is not eating and drinking, but righteousness and peace and joy in the Holy Spirit. 18 For he who in this {way} serves Christ is acceptable to God and approved by men.* (NAS)

2 Cor 10:18 *For not he who commends himself is approved, but whom the Lord commends.*(NAS)

2 Tim 2:15 *Be diligent to present yourself approved to God as a workman who does not need to be ashamed,*

handling accurately the word of truth. (NAS)

I realize that I chance being called harsh at this point but the principles of God and the character of God are what the Kingdom power of God operates on. When Kingdom order and principles are in operation the results are proportionate to the miracles that Jesus had when He proclaimed to the delivered persons "the Kingdom of God has come unto you" (Mt 12:28; Lk 10:9). God will not entertain unclean, impure vessels. I didn't say "imperfect" vessels. If God stopped using imperfect vessels He wouldn't have anything to use. I said "impure" vessels. There is a big difference.

VI. LIFESTYLE

Prayer life — I'm sorry folks, but that's where we've got to start. You don't have to read very far to find that prayer was an overwhelming factor in God's moving at Azusa Street. There is one band of people saying, "Revival is coming -- and God's awesome and He's the Arbiter of the universe and He's sovereign -- so revival is coming -- there's nothing you can do to keep it from coming." Then there is another camp saying, "You've got to pray night and day – you've got to go with out food and water '300 days' out of the year to see revival." God is probably standing in the middle saying, "I want to get you two married. I am sovereign and it's going to happen, but you better be prepared and get your vessel cleaned up if you desire to be a viable part of this time in history." Isa 38:1 *"Thus says the LORD, 'Set your house in order"* ("house": 1004 bayith- human bodies (figurative); household affairs; on the inside; within (B-D-B).

Ps 50:23 *"He who offers a sacrifice of thanksgiving honors me; and to him who orders {his} way {aright} I shall show the salvation of God."* (NAS)

Eph 4:22-24 *that, in reference to your former manner of life, you lay aside the old self, which is being corrupted in accordance with the lusts of deceit, 23 and that you be renewed in the spirit of your mind, 24 and put on the new self, which in {the likeness of} God has been created in righteousness and holiness of the truth.* (NAS)

Titus 2:12 *It teaches us to say "No" to ungodliness and worldly passions, and to live self-controlled, upright and godly lives in this present age,.... 15 These, then, are the things you should teach. Encourage and rebuke with all authority. Do not let anyone despise you.*(NIV)

VII. BECOMING METHODISTS

Perhaps we would all do well to become Methodists. The method that John and Charles Wesley had was: prayer and Bible reading lead to sanctification. We've got to give the Holy Spirit something to work through to bring about the completeness of His dealings in our lives. What's the best thing to give Him to work through? The Word. In fact that's the only thing He will work through. Phil 2:16 *holding fast the word of life, so that in the day of Christ I may have cause to glory because I did not run in vain nor toil in vain.*(NAS) ("holding fast"1907 epecho- to apply, to observe, to attend to; to give attention to)

Isa 66:2 .... *"But to this one I will look, to him who is humble and contrite of spirit, and who trembles at My word.*(NAS)

Heb 4:12 *For the word of God is living and active and sharper than any two-edged sword, and piercing as far as the division of soul and spirit, of both joints and marrow, and able to judge the thoughts and intentions of the heart.*(NAS)

If the Word is down on the inside of us, guess where the Spirit is going to be working. He will be working on that thing the Word is in.

Ps 119:8 *I shall keep Thy statutes; do not forsake me utterly! 9 How can a young man keep his way pure? By keeping {it} according to Thy word. 10 With all my heart I have sought Thee; do not let me wander from Thy commandments. 11 Thy word I have treasured in my heart, that I may not sin against Thee. 12 Blessed art Thou, O LORD; teach me Thy statutes.*(NAS)

VIII. TRY STARTING IT WITHOUT A BATTERY

If a person got away from God's Word (and that is how one would get into error), what basis would the Holy Spirit have for using them? Every believer must give themselves to prayer and the Word but especially those who desire to speak the word of the Lord to others and those who want to go beyond the limits of their past experiences. The Word is what the Holy Spirit works His works with in our life and prayer is that focused time He can do it. Azusa Street was the awesome move of God that it was because, in large part, it was a praying movement. They started prayer before services.

I've had this said to me and I met another minister recently who has had it said to him that "You don't have to do all that praying, just minister out of your gift." I can only imagine what someone would receive from a person who didn't pray but only "ministered out of their gift." That would be tantamount to saying, "Go to the West Coast in that car with the run-down battery. It has an ignition, doesn't it? Well, just use the ignition. Don't worry about the battery."

1Thes 5:17 *PRAY WITHOUT CEASING.*(KJV)

Eph 6:18*With all prayer and petition pray at all times in the Spirit, and with this in view, be on the alert with all perseverance and petition for all the saints,*(NAS)

Jude 1:20 *But you, beloved, building yourselves up on your most holy faith; praying in the Holy Spirit;*(NAS)

IX. THE PREVENTATIVE/EMPOWERING SOLUTION

Imagine Father looking on us and thoughtfully considering the region and ministry and lifestyle we are involved in for the purpose of making an evaluation of it all. Decisions will follow the evaluation which will affect an entire group of people who have supposedly given themselves to a common cause, which is supposedly paramount in all their considerations. And, just think, those decisions could have been averted – there was an on-going involvement that would have made that particular decision-making session totally unnecessary. That is just what happened in Is 59:16 *And He saw that there was no man **and wondered**....* The New American Standard uses this terminology: ***and was astonished** that there was no one to intercede.* It's hard for me picture God sitting on His throne and wondering, "Why don't I have an intercessor? Why is no man praying?" I have queried as to whether He might have even asked aloud to the angels in His wondering: "Angels, help me here. Why don't I have an intercessor in Israel who will step into this situation as representative of *My* heart's cry?"

Of all the things God could possibly wonder about, the Bible tells us He was wondering where His interceding people were. Actually, I don't remember anything else in the Bible that allows us to know that God has ever wondered about any other matter. ("wondered" 8074 shamem- to be desolate, to be appalled, to stun, to stupefy;

to be deflowered, to be deserted, to be appalled, causing horror (Brown-Driver-Briggs) Could it actually be that this God who loved Israel so much felt "deserted" or that the Arbiter of the universe was actually "stunned" or maybe even "stupefied" that people who knew His precepts and had heard His voice so clearly through His prophets could possibly leave His beloved Israel uncovered from lack of prayer? While we have a great host of people who want to speak for God and prophesy (some volunteering to prophesy judgment and doom), where are those falling on their face and interceding?

1 Tim 2:1 *I exhort therefore, that, first of all, supplications, prayers, intercessions, and giving of thanks, be made for all men*; (KJV)

X. BOTH COMPONENTS

We don't just get out there and prophesy and proclaim "thus saith the Lord." Prayer and prophesying go hand in hand. They are two sides to the same coin and both sides are necessary. It's like epoxy: if you have only one of the ingredients in epoxy you don't have anything but a sticky mess. But if you put them together and mix them thoroughly, you've got something that's going to hold some pieces together. You've got something that's going to weather the storm. Just stick one of the components of the epoxy on that leak in the bottom of your boat and see how long your little boat stays together in the middle of the storm. I don't want to be out there in a boat that has been put together with only one component of a two-part solution. I want both components. The other component is called a catalyst. (A catalyst "increases the rate of a reaction; one that precipitates a process or event.") Prayer precipitates God's processes and events.

Num 11:2 *And the people cried unto Moses; and **when Moses prayed** unto the LORD, the fire was quenched.*(KJV)

Job 42:10 *And the LORD turned the captivity of Job, when he prayed for his friends: also the LORD gave Job twice as much as he had before.* (KJV)

Acts 4:31 *After they prayed, the place where they were meeting was shaken. And they were all filled with the Holy Spirit and spoke the word of God boldly.* (NIV)

Acts 6:6 *And these they brought before the apostles; **and after praying**, they laid their hands on them.* (NAS)

Acts 13:3 *Then, when they had fasted and prayed and laid their hands on them, they sent them away.* (NAS)

Acts 14:23 *And **when** they had appointed elders for them in every church, **having prayed** with fasting, they commended them to the Lord in whom they had believed*(NAS)

XI. ONE JOLT TO GO, PLEASE

Thank God for the apostles of prayer who have arisen in the last 10 to 20 years to remind the church that they are supposed to be praying. Every time the people of God have lost something over the course of time God has been determined to restore it. He is a God of restoration. And every time God restores something to the church He has to bring it back in an earthshaking fashion for it to do staid, cynical humans any good. A plain old vitamin B tablet won't get the job done when a virus has our entire system run down. God has to give us a powerful concentration of B in shot form. When the battery goes dead, a simple 10 amp charger isn't enough to get the vehicle going again. A 250amp charger is required and, boy, is there ever a difference between a 10amp spurt of electricity and a 250amp jolt!

Oral Roberts took flack as God used him to help restore healing ministry to the Body of Christ. Dad Hagan has faced difficulties and misunderstanding so the church could regain its revelation of the word and faith. Larry Lee exposed himself to some bumps and bruises as Father used him to begin drawing our hearts back to prayer. Dr. Bill Hamon faced the disdain of brethren as he was used to bring our attention to the value of prophesying for the church today. There are people in this earth now who are willing to stand up to the Jezebels of this age and blaze trails for those aspects of Almighty God that are to be revealed in this hour no matter what jolt they may receive.

XII. WHO'S ON WATCH?

The scripture says that He wondered that there was no intercessor. On occasion I have heard this question: "Why is there evil? Why does God allow 'this' to happen? Why does God allow 'that' to continue?" Perhaps if we read Gen 1:26 we might begin to understand the part that responsible sons play in this realm by way of delegated authority.

Gen 1:26 *Then God said, "Let Us make man in Our image, according to Our likeness; and let them rule over the fish of the sea and over the birds of the sky and over the cattle and over all the earth, and over every creeping thing that creeps on the earth."* (NAS)

Gen 1:28*And God blessed them; and God said to them, "Be fruitful and multiply, and fill the earth, and subdue it; and rule over the fish of the sea and over the birds of the sky, and over every living thing that moves on the earth."* (NAS) ("dominion": 7287 radah (raw-daw') to tread down, i.e. subjugate; prevail against, reign; rule (over), take.) (Strong's Concordance)

("subdue": 3533 kabash (kaw-bash'); to tread down; to conquer, subjugate, violate: KJV-- bring into bondage, force, keep under, subdue, bring into subjection.)

Considering the above definitions of God's original (and unchanged) intention, it would appear that we have a mission laid out before us with authority to get it done. Scripture offers the understanding that the Last Adam has won back all that the first Adam forfeited. Could it be that God actually is not responsible for evil happenings since He handed over the earth to Adam to "subjugate," "prevail against," "reign," "tread down" and "keep under"?

Matt 8:27 *And the men marveled, saying, "What kind of a man is this, that even the winds and the sea obey Him?"* (NAS)

Matt 9:8 *But when the multitudes saw {this,} they were filled with awe, and glorified God, who had given such authority to men.*(NAS)

Luke 10:17 *And the seventy returned with joy, saying, "Lord, even the demons are subject to us in Your name." 18 And He said to them, "I was watching Satan fall from heaven like lightning. 19 "Behold, I have given you authority to tread upon serpents and scorpions, and over all the power of the enemy, and nothing shall injure you.* (NAS)

The question has been pondered, "Where is God in all of this?" It appears that God is in the same position He has always been in…. *wondering why there is no man to intercede.* Our prayers and intercessions are the Father's access into the realm we have dominion in. No wonder Paul commands us to *pray without ceasing.* There is much which needs tending on our watch. This Delegator of Authority is waiting for us to give him the opportunity to act in the realm that He turned over to us.

The Bible reveals the reason why Jesus was manifest: in order that He might destroy the works of the devil. We don't learn that bit of exactness until the Epistle of John. But Jesus has already announced that His disciples are sent into the world just as He was sent.

I Jn 3:8 ....*The Son of God appeared for this purpose, that He might destroy the works of the devil.* (NAS)

John 17:18 *"As Thou didst send Me into the world, I also have sent them into the world.* (NAS)

The Father sent the Son to destroy the works of the devil and the Son has sent us to do likewise.

Chapter Fifteen
Ministry

I. FATHER = SUPPORTIVE STRENGTH

My height barely enabled me to reach his waist so that he towered over me like a giant. I was just a little boy whose curiosity about lawnmowers and cutting grass had reached an unrestrainable zenith. Watching my dad mow the grass wasn't enough. He was my hero and I wanted to do what he did. From my vantage point, mowing grass seemed like one of the greatest things a fellow could possibly do.

After begging my dad many times to let me mow, he finally gave over to a compromise which was a whole lot better than my original idea of mowing by myself. He was very concerned that I not cut off my foot or get hit by anything that the mower might throw. That big mower had a cross-bar for support halfway up the handle. He let me hold on to the crossbar and he towered over me in control of the mower while holding to the main portion of the handle at the top.

I remember the experience quite well for it was my first time to "handle" a powerful motorized machine. In consideration of me, he walked very slowly and carefully watched the location of my feet every moment. The feeling of power was intoxicating. I was pushing that mower and grass was flying all over the place. That mower was moving ahead of me through grass almost to my knee and I was following and walking on a fresh mowed mat. Something delightful was being accomplished and I was part of making it happen with a powerful machine.

After a couple of passes across the yard, which I remember as being about three miles wide, I looked up to my dad to see if he noticed how great I was doing. He did. Only now do I realize that he was doing all the work. He was supplying all the strength. When I think of "father" I think of supportive strength.

Great things were being accomplished not because I was pushing the mower, not because I was doing anything but because he was doing it all. I wasn't really even concerned about where the mower should go. I didn't even understand what made the grass fly forcefully out the side of the mower. In fact, I don't doubt that I was in the way and holding back progress but it didn't seem to matter to him. He was willing to allow me to have part in an exciting adventure. This was my first lesson among many others that would enable me to eventually mow in a proper and capable manner.

My heavenly Father knows my weaknesses and strengths. He is well aware that even my greatest strengths are not enough to accomplish what is needed in that big, sometimes overwhelming, yard called ministry. *As a father has compassion on his children, so the Lord has compassion on those who fear Him; for He knows how we are formed, He remembers that we are dust* (Ps.103:13-14).

Some fear that after having been called or gifted in an area that they will not be able to fulfill it. The fact that they will not be able to fulfill it is true but the fear is not necessary for God will fulfill it. Some are trying to push big mowers they were never called to push. Some are standing up against big yards they were never called to stand against.

If God calls us to push a certain "mower," He will tower over us and do the pushing. All we have to do is obediently walk along and rejoice in the results. Cf. *Yet he did not waver through unbelief regarding the promise of God, but was strengthened in his faith and gave glory to God, being fully persuaded that God had power to do what He had promised* (Rom.4:20-21).

II. BEING AND DOING BY THE ENABLING OF THE HOLY SPIRIT

AS LONG AS WE PRETEND TO BE SOMETHING WE ARE NOT, WE WILL NEVER BE WHAT WE ARE SUPPOSED TO BE. When we are called, we are not called to be something or someone we are not. God wants to use what He has made us by the enabling of the Holy Spirit. (cf. Acts 10:38) Ministry is offered, not forced. God won't put your arm behind your back and force you into it; nor will God obliterate your personality to use you. He will use your personality if it is submitted to His Lordship.

Sometimes folks get all upset about what they feel God might try to make them do. That, however, may be no more than a reaction to people who have tried to obligate or intimidate them into some type of religious busy work. Believe it or not, God will work with your personality, your likes and dislikes. God does not delight in rubbing your nose in them in spite of some, who in your past, may have.

III. CALLING AND EQUIPPING

If David is called upon to face Goliath, it is not without preparation — preparation of will, spirit and the proper skills. David had already faced a bear and a lion and, besides, he was already skilled with a slingshot! In the face of considering fear let us realize that if God calls, God equips. Even the princess and half the kingdom are not enough for me to go out against Goliath (1 Sam. 17:25). In fact, it might just take Gabriel and a few of the boys coming and playing "Onward Christian Soldiers" before I would even consider it!

Realize also that God did not send out David against Goliath just to prove a point. It was all part of the preparation God was doing in David's life while he was on his way to the throne of Israel. Who better should be king than he whose heart was stirred to face nine feet of uncircumcised Philistine because that Philistine dare mock his God? There was no demand on David to face these incredible odds. But David could not have been held back by wild horses! Not even the disbelief which dominated the Israelite army nor the jibes of his own brothers could dissuade what God had flamed in his heart. It was not some form of mere obligation that carried David out in that valley to face those odds. God had already placed the impetus there by placing a love of Himself and a love for Israel in David's heart before he ever heard of Goliath.

IV. WILLINGNESS AND HEART

A story was related to me about a mother washing her clothes at a riverbank in Africa. Suddenly, she heard terrifying screams that she immediately recognized as her four year old daughter. As she sprang to her feet she noticed a very large alligator had her baby in its jaws swimming out into the river. While several men stood nearby also screaming, she ran as fast as possible to her daughter. The mother grabbed the girl's arms and began to tug fiercely against the power of the animal in waist-deep water. After several minutes of wrestling with a determined mother whose heart was in the battle, the confused and frustrated alligator opened his jaws and quietly swam out of sight. Though she had never attended an alligator wrestling school, that mother had a willingness to deal with the matter because her heart was in it. Ministry is not a strain. God gives us the heart for what we are supposed to be and the power to be it at the time He appoints.

V. READY TO.... OR READY NOT TO.....

IT TAKES JUST AS MUCH CONSECRATION TO BE SET ASIDE FOR AWHILE as it does to say "God, I'm ready to put it all on the line." It is all God's ministry and He is perfectly right in using us all the time, some of the time, now and then or not at all or, perphaps, even quietly use us.

In spite of the perception of "ministry" that some of us have come to by observing those "in the know," sometimes we just need to be there for someone or several someones. We don't necessarily have to say anything. But of course, that would require quite a confidence in God to be God for us to simply stand or sit nearby without saying something. As ambassadors (2Co.5:20) or representatives of God, our presence in a situation represents him. Sometimes when we say something, it is simply because we feel pressured to come up with some verbiage and at a moment like that it can be awkward or even the wrong thing to say.

I suppose it would take a certain amount of faith for some of us to just be there and believe that our representation of God in that situation was enough. I'm not sure I can remember one time when a rote statement or a pat answer brought the relief the speaker intended. Recalling the last half of the decade of the 70's when my Dad was terminally ill from cancer, my family just wanted to see people and to know that they cared. We weren't waiting with bated breath for person after person to come and preach us a sermon and quote scriptures they had memorized for just such on occasion. Something from the heart that had been life to them would have been nice; or a fresh word of knowledge given by the Holy Spirit would have been gladly welcomed.

Perhaps some of the time that people call us or call for us to come, it isn't because they want to hear us say things or see us do things, but it is mostly that they gain comfort from our being there because of what we have come to mean to them in relationship or representation and, believe it or not, that is a valid ministry. Once I was called to the home of a couple who had not been physically able to attend church services for a number of years. He was in his nineties and she in her eighties, both of them delightful children of God inspite of very frail bodies. I didn't have to preach, sing or read the Bible. All I had to do was show up and it meant so much to them. However, after that visit along with several others, I was convinced that I was the one who had been ministered to.

VI. THE KEY

The key to ministry is "such as I have, give I thee"(Acts 3:6). Don't try to be something you are not and don't put off ministry until you are able to do it like your favorite TV evangelist. Ministry doesn't need a pulpit to come forth - just a channel. Ministry is the impartation of the Holy Spirit through us. The key question is not "Are you in the ministry?" but "Is ministry in you?" It's easy to submit to Him and be used of Him if we want what he wants.

Ministry is simply taking what God has given you for someone else and giving it to them. You don't have to strain and try to muster up something for the moment. It may be something that God worked in you sometime in the past. There could be a nugget or a rhema word that Father blessed you with once before that is just what this person needs now. The Holy Spirit actually does bring things to our remembrance for a purpose (Jn 14:26). I knew a person once who felt they had to come up with something in every situation they walked into because they had a "reputation" of being prophetic. This person would bring a raised level of anxiety into a room when they walked in because they were so stressed and determined to come up with "a word."

VII. NO SWEAT

It is not apparent from scripture that Jesus walked around in a strain all the time. Ministry came out of who He was in the Father and came as a result of His time with the Father and, if you'll excuse the expression, it seemed to come quite "naturally." When you go to a store because you need something and someone on the other side of the counter hands you what you need, it is quite a "natural" thing for them to get it from the shelf and hand it to you. They are able to do it so "naturally" because it is readily available to them. That's all we have to do: just simply give to others what God has given us for them. The gifts the Holy Spirit uses us in are not our gifts; they are gifts for others and all we have to do is release them.

Chapter Sixteen

Prophetic Boxes

The large, sharp-toothed fish made a mad dash at the minnows only to be rudely awakened to the fact that there was a thick piece of glass between him and a much-desired meal. When a university was conducting some behavioral experiments, they put a Northern Pike in a tank to study his reactions to a set of predetermined circumstances. I have read that the Pike is a veracious eater and he strikes with lightning speed. The full-grown fish was first placed in the large experimental tank by himself. He stayed in the tank for several days and was allowed to swim about freely. After a couple of days of going without food, the researchers placed a piece of glass in the tank which divided it in half. On the opposite end of the tank from the Pike, they placed a couple dozen minnows - the Pike's favorite food. As soon as they hit the water and began to move about, the Pike rushed at them with bullet speed. He crashed into the glass and was cast into a great deal of confusion. The hungry Northern gathered himself and made another sudden rush at the minnows and was again rudely halted by the glass which he could not see. After attempting several times to reach the minnows he so desired, the Pike gave up and swam to the opposite end of the tank and simply watched the delectable morsels swimming freely in the opposite end. The researchers then removed the glass partition and the minnows began to swim about the full length of the tank. Some of the minnows even bumped into the large fish but were allowed to go on about their ambling and maneuvering without being accosted. My understanding is that the fish died in that tank with food swimming all about him. It would seem that the behavioral discovery made in this particular instance shows us that if Northern Pikes are repeatedly denied access to their favorite food, their behavior pattern changes so radically that they will starve even once their ardent desire is granted (which in this case was access to a food source).

ALTERED BEHAVIOR

It is interesting that studies of animal behavior patterns can also give us a glimpse into the behavior of humans. I believe the common denominator is the fact that God has placed within all living beings certain drives and desires that enable us to get to the goals He has for each of us. For animals that basic goal is to multiply and fill the earth and take their place in the ecological chain. For people that basic goal is to have dominion in the earth in such a way that it brings glory to our Creator and Father. It should be quite obvious that our Creator has meant for Northern Pike to regularly enjoy the flavor of lake minnows. But when that Pike wholeheartedly throws himself into fulfilling that natural drive within him and is sufficiently thwarted on more than one occasion, he builds a "new box" for his beliefs and subsequently adopts new behavior patterns.

The experience the Northern had with the glass partition convinced him that it was time for a "paradigm shift." A paradigm is an example that serves as a pattern or a model. If a person has a certain type of experience in a certain set of circumstances, they will typically expect that very same experience each time they encounter that same set of circumstances. An older man once told me about a dog which he watched walk down a sidewalk on a daily basis. The dog would come down the same sidewalk every day at the same time. As the animal approached this man's place of business, the dog would raise his leg and, in animal fashion, mark the large post which held up the sign advertising the services of the gentleman's business. On one particular day, the electrically lighted sign had developed an electrical short to everyone's surprise. The dog came down the very same sidewalk at the very same time and in typical fashion raised his leg and began to mark his territory. But on this particular day, the normal set of circumstances had been altered by unpredicted elements. When the liquid stream contacted the sign post the dog received a sudden shock. Much amused, the old gentleman allowed me to know that the befuddled canine never attempted to mark that post again. However, the dog would come down the street until he was somewhat near the post, look up at the post, completely cross over to the other side of the street, and after walking a few yards on the opposite side of the street, he would cross back over and continue his journey on down the sidewalk.

There are many experiences which we have in life that have altered our behavior. In a good many cases it is probably wise that we have learned from them. But in some cases we have allowed our experiences in particular situations to dictate changes to us which have in turn affected our destiny. Some of those effects will not be immediate but they hold long-term results for us. Some of us have had experiences where we have trusted God in certain matters and when expected results did not take place, we stopped believing God in those areas. There have been instances when we trusted in Christians and in ministers who let us down and we adjusted our behavior for future reference. There are people who were once convinced that they had a true prophecy from God or that they had received a burden or a vision from God that was their life's call and nothing ever materialized on the matter. When that happens we determinedly embrace a "paradigm shift" and woe be to anyone who tries to talk: us out of it. Once we were convinced that God's intentions toward us were large but because we experienced a repeated hindrance, we now believe we never did hear from God. And like the Pike, when that which we ardently desired finally is swimming all about us, and even bumping up against us, we starve because we now believe in our experience more than we believe the word of the Lord.

AN UNEXPECTED FORM

How many times has the Word accomplished in our lives what it was sent to accomplish but it came in a form we didn't expect? There is a story I have heard since I was a boy about a man who lived near a river. There came a great flood and the water rose up high on the house chasing him up onto the roof He began to pray and cry out, "God rescue me!" A helicopter came and they called out over the loud speaker, "Grab the rope and climb up." He thanked them but refused because he was "waiting for God to rescue him." People came in a boat and he refused them also. Finally the rushing water swept the house away and him along with it and he drowned. When he got to Heaven, as the story goes, he was asked why he refused the helicopter and the boat which the Lord had sent.

Peter had yielded his life to God to be used in whatever way God desired and when God attempted to send him to Cornelius, a Gentile, Peter began to call all the things in the sheet "unclean." God sternly instructed Peter not to call unclean what He had called clean (Acts 10:15). In order to cooperate with an unprecedented move of God among the Gentiles, Peter had to let God out of the little box he had built for Him. God burst into Peter's neat little paradigm and demanded change if Peter was going to be able to participate.

It appears obvious to me why satan is stirring up so much negative reaction to prophecy and prophetic ministries. We all have paradigms that must be changed in order to embrace and be part of what God is doing at the end of this age. Prophetic accuracy will build bridges to the new paradigm that we must embrace in order to go on to the next stage of purpose in fully realizing our destiny. There are so-called "full Gospel" people proposing resolutions right now for their denomination to adopt that proclaim that they do not believe in predictive prophecy nor do they believe in impartation by the laying on of hands. The first time such a resolution was proposed it was as a reaction to certain abuses pointed at the Latter-Rain movement in the late '40's. So, the inference here, as I understand it, is: If prophecy and prophetic ministers tend to be problematic, let's throw out prophecy and prophetic people no matter the instruction of Scripture; and let's build an airtight theological box that both keeps certain things in and certain things out regarding this subject. (Cf. 1 Tim 4:14).

The enemy is fighting the prophetic word so vehemently because prophetic words will change a person's paradigm. When Joseph had that predictive, prophetic dream there was no evidence anywhere in his environment, that would even so much as hint, that some day he would be a father to Pharaoh (Gen 45:8). In David's case, how could a lowly shepherd become the king of Israel? The dream of Joseph and the prophet pouring oil on David's head began to change their paradigm. Those prophetic impartations began to burst their little inadequate boxes completely apart. There is a lively element to prophecy that cannot leave us like we are. That God-thing on the inside of us begins to get into agreement with His Word and makes room for His Word to come alive in us and work in us what otherwise was impossible before. The reason I like to use the eagle as a symbol of the prophetic is because of what the eagle represents to us: the ability to rise above; the ability to soar high and see from God's perspective. The prophetic word enables us to rise up and see what we were not able to see from our circumstances.

God uses prophecy to break into our paradigms. "For My thoughts are not your thoughts, neither are your ways My ways, " declares the LORD. "For {as} the heavens are higher than the earth, so are My ways higher than your ways, and My thoughts than your thoughts. "For as the rain and the snow come down from heaven, and do not return there without watering the earth, and making it bear and sprout, and furnishing seed to the sower and bread to the eater; So shall My word be which goes forth from My mouth; it shall not return to me empty, without accomplishing what I desire, and without succeeding {in the matter} for which I sent it. (Isa 55:8-11, NAS) His superior (and without limitation) thoughts break into our finite (and limited) thoughts and are therefore empowered to accomplish His purposes. We continually demand that God fit into our paradigm and God is continually trying to get us into His paradigm (C£ Phil 1 :6). Do you want a larger experience in God? Then you must allow God to enlarge your revelation. We cannot operate beyond our revelation.

It seems that God even had a tough time delivering Israel from slavery. You would think that anyone would want to be delivered from slavery and given half a chance, would take it. Whenever Israel came up against a tough spot, they wanted to go back to Egypt which obviously meant that they would be returning to slavery. They claimed that they wanted to return to the leeks and garlic they had eaten in Egypt. They presented the "leeks and garlic" argument as though that was something to shoot for in life. However, it wasn't that it was a worthy goal to be obtained, it was that they had been jerked out of their 400 year old paradigm and and now things were just too different for them. Leeks and garlic should be merely garnishes, not a full meal. God was trying to get Israel to a land flowing with milk and honey and they were stuck with a taste for leeks and garlic. They were determined to stay on a diet of mere staples (bare necessities, basics) and God was trying to give them rich delicacies. They had to get past Num 25:1 (Shittim) and cross through Jordan and die to self's paradigm. What self-imposed limitations can I die to today? What assumed limitations can I die to today?

THE PARADIGM OF THE WORD

How many times has the Word of God accomplished in our lives what it was sent to accomplish but it came in a form we didn't expect? Ask the Pharisees what it is like to reject a Messiah who came from God but didn't look just exactly like they required Him to look. We can look back on the Scriptures and ask, "How on earth could those dense people miss their Messiah?" Yet, we get our "law" refined, build our fences of containment on exact lines and add our personal little nuances to it; and by the time we get through and our disciples get through throwing their part in, we begin to call "this" and "that" "not God." It wouldn't be near as bad if we would only say "this" or "that" is not of God but then we just have to go and say "he" or "she" is not of God.

The Scriptures will build bridges to the new paradigm we need if we will get back to biblical theology rather than traditional or experiential theology.

PLATO'S CAVE

Men have a most difficult time adjusting to new or different concepts. People think that they are right and that their paradigm is THE paradigm and tend to go about attempting to get others to embrace their paradigm. Hence, a good reason to have a paradigm or a "box" that we are continually about the business of enlarging. After all, the revelation of an infinite God must be growing in us or we stalemate. Plato told a story of a group of people who had been imprisoned in a cave. It seems that these people were shackled in such a way that they could see the shadows of the outside world on the back wall of the cave but they could not see out of the cave to confirm the meaning of the shadows. They would conjecture and theorize what each shadow meant. It appeared that one shadow represented a man and his horse. They decided that a multiple figured shadow was a circus going by and on and on they went coming to conclusion after conclusion as to what the shadows meant. One day a member of their group managed to escape his bonds and flee. When the man got free of the confines of the cave, he discovered that the shadows they had seen on the cave wall did not at all represent the things they had thought they represented. After a period of time the escapee felt that he should return to the captives and tell them how wrong they had all been about the shadows. He did return and when he tried to explain that they had been wrong and what the shadows actually represented, they jumped him and killed him. They did not like to think that they had been wrong, especially since they were in such a condition.

One woman considers weeping through an entire service insanity and yet for another it is breaking through years of hurts and disillusionment to freedom. Laughing for one person is foolishness while for another it is the release of years of captivity in anger and bitterness. For one long-time Pentecostal the remark is, "What's the big deal? I don't see any purpose for gold dust." For a person who has only been walking with the Lord for a couple of years, they are greatly humbled and with tears running down their cheeks they ask, "Why would God love me so much that He would leave the residue of His Presence on me like this?" Some have spoken out against people who have jerked, sometimes violently, in outpouring meetings. Recently I jerked a number of times in a meeting. It was like a strong electrical shock and my arm and leg suddenly flew up into the air. I asked God, "What is this about?" He dropped into my heart a reminder that He is letting me know that I am not in charge.

RADICAL CHANGE

Though some of us desperately long for the routine of our lives to be radically changed, we are disturbed and consequently resistant when confronted with the acts of God's power which are required to change them. Our assumptions of what it will take and what we will stand for must be transformed by a divine encounter with the Holy Spirit. For all that we receive from God is by the power of the Holy Spirit (Acts 2:33; Rom.lS:13 by the power of the Spirit).

So, in order for God to radically change the present state of the church and the present state of our personal lives, we must allow Him to forcefully break in upon us! There were 500 people who were commanded to wait for the Promise of the Father in Jerusalem. There were 380 who did not allow God to forcefully break in upon their lives and only got to read about the 120 who did.

BUILDING BOXES FOR GOD TO GET IN

One material we build boxes out of which we demand God to get into is our prayers. We pray in very specific terms and then expect God to show up and do that which is within the parameters of those terms. A most human tendency is to pray in such a way that we are ordering God around like we would a bellboy in some hotel. God is not just sitting around awaiting our orders. God is on the move (He is always dynamic and never static) and doing what He can to align us with-His purposes. As mentioned earlier, how many times has God answered our prayers but the .... answer came in a form we were not expecting? There have been times when we have accused God of not answering prayer but then a year or so later we discover that He did. It just so happens that the answer came in a different wrapper or down an avenue we had not been looking for it to come down. From our limited perspectives, we cry out in with limited understanding and emotionally demand specifics of God - many of which He may not be able to agree because they are out of alignment with the principles of His Word. God will not get into alignment with fear or greed.

Our default modes are another way in which we present God with boxes for Him to maneuver in. We can come to some freedom, some fresh revelation that has us out and beyond where we have ever been, and be doing just fine as we go along the road of purpose. Then an unexpected, or a much feared, occurrence blows into the middle of the scene and stuff is flying up in our face obscuring our vision and throwing us off balance. The carnal thing we do so well at this point is: we fall back on old defaults. It is somewhat like this analogy: Say a man has only used an ax or a bow and arrow to meet the food needs of his large family. He manages to get a few animals now and then with his ax and his bow but it is very difficult hunting and he is not always successful. Then someone comes along and gives him a gun with plenty of bullets. Now he doesn't have to spend as much time hunting and he is able to get the game he needs with much less effort. But one day, just as he is getting used to this new gun, he makes a mistake, it misfires and blows up in his hands and wounds him. After depending on the ax and bow for so many years and not being wounded by either one, he will most likely go into his default mode. He will throw the gun away and go back to his ax and bow even though the gun has proven to be a far superior means of obtaining his family's needs.

I know of situations where pastors who have come into revelation of what prophecy can do in people's lives, have shut down all prophecy in their church because they lost some people over prophecy or over a mistake a prophetic minister made in their church. There are people who have zealously believed in divine healing and because someone whom they loved was not healed, they went back to the default of "God heals some and doesn't heal others." They then begin to teach that "the ultimate healing is death." God will not get into agreement with our disappointments.

EXPERIENCE = THEOLOGY?

In a circus environment there is not much room for eight ton elephants. Not only are these animals very large, they are also very strong and able to do a lot of damage if they get loose. There is a method which trainers use to keep elephants in a small confined area. It seems that there is a very good reason for huge elephants staying put in one little place with a little chain around their leg in the confines of a circus environment. All of this is done without great, thick cement walls and it takes very little room. When the elephant is a baby, a trainer drives a stake into the ground and puts a chain on the elephant's leg and then attaches it to the stake. The baby typically does not like it and begins to pull against the chain but is unable to do anything about it. As he grows larger and stronger, he never tries to pull up the stake again because he was convinced at one point that it would do no good to try and get free. The moment he feels resistance, he relents. His experience becomes his theology.

CHANGING OUR PARADIGMS

God instructs us in Scripture to change our

paradigms: Enlarge the place of your tent; stretch out the curtains of your dwellings, spare not; Lengthen your cords, and strengthen your pegs. For you will spread abroad to the right and to the left. And your descendants will possess nations, and they will resettle the desolate cities. (Isa 54:2-3 NAS) It is interesting to note that when we stretch out and enlarge our willingness to perceive, and hence ability to receive, then our descendants will be able to possess and accomplish what has not been possessed and accomplished in the past.

God will always be bigger than your theology. We will never have a theology big enough to fully encompass God. No matter how well built our little boxes are, no matter what fine intentions or materials have built them, they will never be big enough or good enough to contain all of God. His thoughts and His ways are above ours, so that tells me that as long as man exists, that he will constantly be amazed at the developing revelation of who God is and what His purposes are.

There will be people with very strong boxes and paradigms that actually will not be able to see or comprehend something that God is doing because God did not do it within the parameters of their paradigm. There are already people looking into the mouths of those who have received gold fillings and proclaiming, "I don't see anything." We have boxes that we expect God to climb into in order to do for us or through us or to us. In coming days we will have to abandon the limitations of those close-quarter points of reference. There is a proportion and a scale that God is determined to operate on and He is determined to get us to that scale and proportion. God may very well have said, "I am not like you" in Ps 50:21." But He is most determined that we shall be like Him (Cf. 2Co 3:18; Rom 8:29; Col3:1O). God's main concern is not to get us to heaven but to get us formed into the image of His Son and since we are bought with the purchase price of the blood of Jesus, it is His right to break out of the little boxes we build.

Strengthen Encourage Equip Comfort

This book is a publication of **SEEC Ministries International** (A Corporation Sole). **SEEC** stands for Strengthen, Encourage, Equip and Comfort according to 1Co 14:3 and Eph 4:12 as taken from the New International Version. This is our mission statement and **SEEC Ministries International** is attempting to accomplish that mission through ministry in local churches, around the globe, in conferences, seminars, through publishing, audio and video. For a catalog listing of the CDs, DVDs, books and manuals available by Marty and Kathy Gabler, send us an e-mail at: mail@seecministries.org or write us at PO Box 298 Coldspring, TX 77331.

SEEC Magazine is published by **SEEC Ministries International**. **SEEC Magazine** is a bi-monthly publication. It is for the purpose of presenting teaching on the subjects of prophecy, five-fold ministry, gifts of the Spirit, dreams and visions, and intercession. Though each of these subjects may not be covered in each issue, they will be covered through the course of the year's publications.

SUBSCRIPTIONS: Please send your name and address to **SEEC Magazine**   PO Box 298 Coldspring,TX 77331. A donation of $15.00/yr. is suggested to help with publication costs.

We would like to send you a free copy of SEEC Magazine. Just contact us at mail@seecministries.org or our PO Box.

A resource catalog is available upon request.

Kingdom Congress is the first Wed.-Fri. of March
each year. Info: **martygabler.com**
Check for devotions and info on
FaceBook: Marty Gabler

**SEEC Ministries International
PO Box 298
Coldspring, TX 77331
seecministries.org
mail@seecministries.org**

Made in the USA
Lexington, KY
01 August 2018